REFLECTIONS
ON THE
NIGERIAN CIVIL WAR

Facing the Future

REFLECTIONS ON THE NIGERIAN CIVIL WAR

Facing the Future

RAPH UWECHUE

New, revised and expanded edition

With Forewords by
Nnamdi Azikiwe & Léopold Sédar Senghor

Africana Publishing Corporation • New York

Published
in the United States of America 1971
by Africana Publishing Corporation
101 Fifth Avenue
New York, N.Y. 10003

Great Britain:
Meier & Holmes Ltd.
18-22 Inverness Street
London N.W.1

© Copyright 1971 Raph Uwechue
All rights reserved

Library of Congress Catalog Card No. 71-105095
I.S.B.N. 0-8419-0037-X

This is a new and revised edition of
Reflections on the Nigerian Civil War. A Call for Realism
published by O.I.T.H. International Publishers Ltd., London, 1969.

Printed in the United States of America

To

The True and Thoughtful African

*The future of this vast country of Nigeria
must depend in the main on the efforts
of ourselves to help ourselves.*

Abubakar Tafawa Balewa
First Prime Minister of Nigeria

CONTENTS

PUBLISHER'S NOTE

This new, revised and expanded edition of the book originally titled *Reflections on the Nigerian Civil War. A Call for Realism* was prompted by the sudden end of the Nigerian civil war. It now includes an account of that war up to the collapse of Biafra.

Two epilogues and a series of portraits of the principal figures involved in the Nigerian conflict have been added. In "The Genesis of Failure" Mr. Uwechue analyses the role played by the Biafran leadership. In "An Elastic Federal Union" he revises and expands upon the proposals initially set forth in chapter 6. An appendix that appeared in the original edition has been deleted in the present book.

The original text, written during the heat of the civil war, embodies much of the passion that inspired the author. This aspect of the work has been preserved.

FOREWORD

by the Rt. Hon. Dr. Nnamdi Azikiwe, P.C.
Former President of the Federal Republic of Nigeria

To write a foreword in a book written during a civil war which
has shocked the conscience of humanity by its savagery and
brutality is not an easy task. Since I am also engaged in preparing
a lengthy study of the military revolution in Nigeria, and the fact
that I was Head of State when the first coup d'etat occurred, I
am emboldened to write frankly and objectively.

The author of this book is a native of Ogwashi-Uku in the
Midwestern state. He was educated at the University of Ibadan,
from where he was graduated with honours in history. He
served for many years in the Nigerian foreign service and opened
that country's diplomatic mission in Paris before the civil war. He
reads, writes and speaks French fluently. He is married and has
four children, three girls and a boy.

This book contains eight chapters: a time for reflection, the
revolution of January 1966, army miscalculations and errors by
politicians, secession and the problem of minorities, intervention
from external sources, proposal for a loose federation of six
states, the army and the nation, the future and a new political
system, embodying suggestions for a new republican constitution. Two appendices incorporate important statements' by leading Nigerians and a number of African Heads of States and

include the decisions reached by the military leaders in Aburi, Ghana, on 4-5 January 1967.

The civil war is now 85 weeks old. It is estimated that during this period 200,000 troops on both sides had died. The United Nations Children's Fund (U.N.I.C.E.F.) has stated that 1.5 million civilians, most of whom were children, have perished in this fratricidal struggle. Various individuals and groups have used their good offices to try to end this awful war, but they did not succeed because of the rigidity of the contestants who have consistently refused to shift their entrenched grounds of contention.

The Commonwealth Secretariat tried to reconcile the two parties. The talks about talks in London and the peace conference in Kampala were not successful because Nigeria insisted that Biafra should fulfill certain conditions and Biafra objected on the ground that they would derogate its assumed sovereignty. When the Commonwealth Prime Ministers met in London, last January, the issue was shelved and was not allowed to be included on the agenda.

Individual citizens of various countries, including those of the United Kingdom, United States of America, and France, have visited both countries in an honest attempt to stop further bloodshed; but they were discouraged by the unwillingness of those concerned to compromise.

For a long time, the United Nations Organization remained aloof. Its Secretary-General, U Thant, asserted that since the issue had not been properly brought to the notice of any of the principal organs of this world body, it would be preferable to leave matters in the hands of the Organization of African Unity which has been handling same since Kinshasa summit of September 1967.

In Mr. Uwechue's opinion, secession is not a solution to the Nigerian crisis because it favoured a particular majority linguistic group. According to his argument, "Claims that many minorities are fighting with Biafra are true. But equally true is the indisputable fact that many of them are fighting against her." Thus he suggests a plebiscite in the disputed areas to enable the inhabitants therein to determine their future political relationship.

Finally, he submits that what was important was that different peoples should agree to live together or agree to separate along clearly defined lines. Nigeria could be made to harbour all the linguistic groups which form its multi-national structure, "by broadening the base upon which our union is founded." He suggests a loose federation to form a sort of United States of Nigeria *based*, with suitable modifications, such as increasing the number of states beyond the original four, *on the Aburi Agreement.*

His main reasons for proposing this type of political association are to save the Ibo-speaking peoples from extermination, on the one hand, and to preserve the territorial integrity of Nigeria, on the other. "Our duty now, if we are to survive," he proposes, "is to create the right conditions for the growth of the right type of leadership capable of wiser investment and better management of our national assets." To achieve this objective, four immediate steps are necessary: suppression of the twelve-state decree and simultaneous renunciation of secession; immediate cease-fire with a mixed force of O.A.U. and Commonwealth contingents to supervise same; establishment of a national relief and rehabilitation body to administer reparations and relief; transfer of power from military personnel to civilians after an accurate census, introduction of births and deaths register, convening of a constituent assembly, and free and fair elections on both regional and national levels.

I commend this book to those who are interested in resolving the Nigerian crisis with realism. The brevity of the chapters and its lucid style of presentation make it a *must* reading for people who are usually bogged down by the responsibilities of office or business or politics. It deserves a kindly reception by observers of international affairs and experts on African studies.

This book should fill an important space in the libraries of those who love the path of peace through just and honourable means based on a realistic approach to human problems.

Nnamdi Azikiwe.

London
27th February 1969.

FOREWORD

by Léopold Sédar Senghor
President of the Republic of Senegal

A Man of Sense and Courage

I am sure, I will be blamed for writing this foreword, especially by the contending parties in Nigeria, less though, no doubt, by General Gowon and Col. Ojukwu themselves than by their hawks. I will be accused of interference, especially as a Head of State, in the "internal affairs" of a "sister-country." But it is precisely because of the fact that this matter concerns a "sister-state" that my intervention ceases to be a crime, or indeed, even a fault but becomes a duty. As Raph Uwechue himself has put it, "In this kind of situation and in the larger interest of Africa and African peoples, to lend an active hand in settling disputes that arise, especially when such disputes lead to large scale bloodshed, cannot be correctly considered as interference."

Of course, I could always say that I am intervening just in my capacity as a writer, as in fact I was requested to do last year by the German writer Günter Grass. But in the present circumstances hiding behind a "literary wall" is not the most courageous thing to do. As a matter of fact, I have already intervened, since 1964, in my capacity as an African Head of State—and this at the request of the two parties, for the differences in Nigeria were not born today. As Uwechue demonstrates, they are essentially a tribal question which dates from independence and beyond.

Indeed, in 1964, on the occasion of my last visit to Nigeria, my two friends—there is no question of denying or disavowing these friendships—President Nnamdi Azikiwe and Prime Minister Sir Abubakar Tafawa Balewa, confided their fears and anxiety to me and requested that I should preach the necessity for maintaining the Federation. This I did both in Lagos and in all the four regions. Such became the case indeed, that, among the English-speaking states in Africa, it was with Nigeria that Senegal had maintained the closest cooperation. It goes beyond that, for, since the secession of Biafra on 30th May 1967, I have received at Dakar, several missions from both parties coming to explain their respective stands in the conflict. It is because Senegal has always refused to take sides with either party, and has always recommended an immediate cease-fire, followed by negotiations with no other pre-condition than the *integrity*—I do not say *unity*—of Nigeria, that the manuscript of Raph Uwechue won me over at once.

Then I said to myself, *here at last, is a man of sense and courage.*

Not, naturally, that I agree with the author in every minute detail of his judgment or his proposals. But he is modest and does not ask that of us. What he proposes to us, after presenting us with a series of verifiable *facts*, is more than just a solution. It is a *method* of finding solutions that are at once just and effective. Herein lies his double merit. Uwechue is a man well informed and consequently objective. He is a man of principle who is at the same time a realist. All through the length of his work, which is clear and brief, we find the combination of practice and theory, of methodical pragmatism and moral rationalism—a characteristic which marks out the very best among the anglophones. The art of presentation itself is very striking.

It is in this tone that the book opens with a preliminary note which gives us certain necessary pieces of information on the history, geography and ethnography of Nigeria. After, comes the preface which indicates the author's objective and exposes the essence of the problem; then chapter I, A Time for Reflection, which in a way summarizes the history of the problem; chapters II and III develop this history while chapters VII and VIII contain concrete proposals for a solution. The work terminates with appendices comprising extracts from historic speeches and the decisions, later to be strongly disputed, reached at the famous *Aburi Conference*.

Before returning to the subject and objective of the author, it should be stated that he was, up till the end of 1968, a member of the Biafran delegation in Paris. He was even—he brings it out in his preface—one of the three diplomats decorated on the occasion of the first anniversary of Biafra's declaration of independence. A few months later he resigned his appointment, *without a quarrel*, nevertheless, with Biafra, after giving his reasons to the Permanent Secretary of the Foreign Office. It is these reasons that constitute the essence of his book and especially of the preface and chapter I, A Time for Reflection.

"This book is intended to play a positive role. Its objective is to plead the cause of peace—the cause of reason." Thus begins the preface.

For Uwechue there is a double objective: (a) to assure the *security of persons and property* first of all, of the Ibos themselves, who seceded with this objective in mind and (b) to build a *confederation* such as was suggested at Aburi.

But a confederation by itself is not his ultimate goal nor is it the *integrity*—not unity—of Nigeria itself, for the sake of *integrity*.

This man of experience and sense who launches an appeal for realism, *a call for realism*, sees very clearly that the only *myth*, like all great myths, which has any embodiment, the only modern ideology which has stood the test of the twentieth century, is the ideology of the *nation*.

For him the *nation* thus appears as the only *ideal* which is capable at one and the same time of gathering and mobilizing the fifty million Nigerians divided into some two hundred and fifty ethnic groups or tribes in order to mould them into a great modern nation.

It is this leading idea, this lucid passion, that leads his argument throughout the length of the manuscript.

And, to begin with, it is this ideal which inspires him and leads him through the first four, more correctly, five chapters which, once more, constitute the history of the problem. Alongside the priority which he gives to the national ideal, the other thing that struck me is the moderation which he brings to bear on his judgment of the protagonists.

He is not the man to forgo his *Iboism*, but because in him this is transcended by a *national will*, he thus acquires the force to judge both facts and men with serene objectivity.

Be it the young officers who organized the coup d'etat of 15th January 1966 or those that the "coup"—as the anglophones call it—of July 1966 brought to the headship of the state, or be it finally, the secession of Biafra, he shows understanding even while he does not approve. Of course, he condemns in turn, and on specific facts, the young military men, General Gowon or Lt. Col. Ojukwu. But the word "condemn" is, in reality, too strong and lacks the attendant attenuating circumstances. While acknowledging a nationalist passion with regard to the young officers of the first coup, he refrains from heaping too much on Gowon and Ojukwu. He presents them to us as men of good will overpowered respectively by their hawks. But even then he does not condemn without giving them a chance of appeal. Thus after having, in chapter II, posed a number of questions concerning General Gowon, he concluded: "I will prefer to leave every Nigerian reader to try to think out the answers for himself or herself. The objective being aimed at in this chapter, which I consider the most important in this book, is to show to fellow

Nigerians and to Nigeria's friends that the principal cause of our current tragedy is *bitterness born of misunderstanding*."

We see the author extremely severe on Nigerian politicians. I would not say that all of them merit this severity but I am with him when he tries to show understanding towards the military protagonists. Naturally the same is not true for other military coups d'etat, most of which, alas! reveal the characteristics of too much politicking.

More surprising to me is his relative moderation vis-à-vis foreign intervention, particularly that of the big powers. This no doubt comes from prudence and legitimate anxiety to safeguard Nigeria's future.

However, Uwechue does not content himself with giving the history of the Nigerian tragedy and apportioning blames. We have even seen that for him this is not of great importance. The essential thing was, and is, to discover and rekindle the national flame from the ashes of misunderstanding. This he sets out to do with his proposals in chapters VII and VIII. Here again, one can distinguish the essential from the secondary or perhaps more correctly the general, which is African, from the particular, which is Nigerian.

The essential are the immediate measures to be taken, the most important among which I mention below:

—abolition of the decree creating the twelve states and simultaneous renunciation of secession;

—an immediate cease-fire with O.A.U. and Commonwealth contingents to enforce it;

—fixing of a date for return to civilian rule;

—an accurate census of the population to be undertaken by United Nations experts;

—the setting up of a constituent assembly;

—submission of the new constitution to a popular referendum;

—organization of elections to the Federal Parliament, as well as to the State Assemblies—this exercise to be entrusted exclusively to the army under the control of O.A.U. and Commonwealth observers.

I shall not stop at the suggestions concerning the "new republican constitution" which appear to me less convincing, in any case less important—no doubt because I have not lived through the Nigerian realities. I shall on the contrary, emphasize the two leading ideas of Uwechue, ideas which he developed in the preface, in chapter I and especially in chapter V. As we all know it is the two interrelated problems of *federation-confederation* and the *number of states* which are at the very roots of the civil war and which, even today, 16th March 1969, block access to negotiation. It is precisely on these problems that our author appears to me to have views which are at once very original, very just and consequently, the most effective in the long run.

With regard to *federation-confederation*, Uwechue by giving them clear definition, very judiciously, transcends the play upon words which, up till now, has masked the reality of these institutions. For him *confederation* excludes *secession* which he presents as a "total separation." It accords less than "absolute sovereignty," as indeed was envisaged by the Aburi Conference. This therefore makes it a *loose federation* such as has always emerged from all consultations held in Nigeria.

It is within the framework of this definition, broad enough and yet precise at the same time, that Uwechue tackles, in chapter V, the problem of *number of states*.

He points out rightly that the question is one of avoiding two extremes: creating as many states as there are 250 tribes, or returning to the former four regions which will in fact, favour the three most populous tribes. "What we should strive for," he concludes, "is a situation in which neither the majority groups (Hausa, Ibo or Yoruba), nor the minority groups are in a position to dominate the entire country."

I am convinced that this book, lucid and courageous, will convince the majority of men of good will. In this respect it merits to be translated into various languages for international diffusion, and first of all into French to cover the whole of Africa. It will contribute to the restoration of peace and advance the birth of a new Nigeria which can occupy the place it merits in Africa, less by its material wealth than by the cultural value of its people.

Léopold Sédar Senghor.

Dakar
16th March 1969.

AUTHOR'S PREFACE

> War is an activity in which the contingent plays an essential part. The results at which it aims can be achieved only if the nature of the enemy is kept constantly in view.
>
> Charles de Gaulle

This book is intended to play a positive role. Its objective is to plead the cause of peace—the cause of reason. Depending on how the situation is viewed by the reader there will be as much to agree with as perhaps to disagree with. It is not written against anyone although what it has to say or perhaps the way it says it may occasionally, but certainly unintentionally, displease certain interested parties. This is because it is not intended to cajole or flatter but to point to bitter realities with a view to urging necessary and urgent corrections. It is not a history book attempting to present every known fact about the current conflict or to analyze such facts in detail. It is essentially a book of advocacy making a case for the cessation of hostilities and for a peaceful settlement of our differences. It is for the consideration not only of the present leadership on both sides but also of the uncommitted public inside and outside Nigeria anxious and willing to see a quick end to the present wasteful and senseless conflict. The main aim is to prick our national conscience or whatever is left of it, to make us stop drifting and start thinking—and thinking not only of past injuries but of practical possibilities for the present and the future. For me by far the most important consideration that should occupy our minds right now is how to save millions of underprivileged and innocent people from untimely death which they did not provoke and which they do not deserve. Our leaders should conscientiously think of these people and reconsider their present rigid positions. The type of courage required of responsible leadership at this moment is moral courage. This is the time for our leaders to show that courage and admit that something has gone gravely wrong, is still going wrong and ought to be quickly arrested.

The views expressed in this book are in favour of a *confederal solution* to the Nigerian problem. To those outside the informed but very limited Biafran circles, it may appear strange that someone who has represented the Biafran cause so seriously for so long and whose humble contribution to that cause earned him an official Biafran decoration (I was one of three diplomats abroad decorated by the Biafran Government on 30th May 1968—the first anniversary of the Declaration of Independence) should now come out so strongly in favour of something short of absolute sovereignty for Biafra. For such readers some explanation is necessary.

For me the principal point at issue on which I disagreed with the Federal Government was its inability, some say its unwillingness (a) to provide effective protection for Ibo civilians during the gruesome massacres of 1966 and (b) its unsatisfactory handling of the question of compensation and rehabilitation of the families and dependents of the victims of those unfortunate events.

My opposition to the Federal Government originated precisely from my reaction against this failure on its part. It was not based on any sudden realization that the Nigerian peoples who had lived together in one country and in that sense, as one community, in considerable harmony for over half a century have become such inveterate incompatibles that they must now be separated in order to be saved. It was thus an opposition against a particular act of a particular government at a crucial time but not against the idea *per se* of one country. As long as this government insisted on conquering instead of calming and compensating the injured Ibos, I was prepared to join forces with anyone to fight for the right of the Ibos to a decent life in adequate security. Whether this was achieved through securing separate sovereignty for the Ibos or through a *confederal arrangement* within Nigeria which guaranteed them their security, was merely a matter of means. It was in this state of mind that I joined the struggle and when secession was declared, despite certain private and personal reservations, I supported it as long as Lagos showed itself unwilling to negotiate or consider a *confederal solution* as outlined in the *Aburi accord*.

For me personally, for numerous reasons which I have tried to show in this book, a *confederal arrangement* had always appeared to be the most realistic solution. Secession, that is total separation, was also equally a means if it could be secured by mutual agreement; otherwise it involved great risks and dangers for both sides. However, as long as it was not possible to secure what in my opinion was the ideal solution for our particular case—a *confederal arrangement*—I would support secession. And so I did.

My support for separate sovereignty for Biafra, therefore, has been all along on this important condition. To the Biafran leadership and to those Biafran friends with whom right from the start, I had constantly exchanged views regarding this unfortunate conflict as a whole, my stand in this respect had always been clear. Within this circle, I had begun to argue openly and with "irritating obstinacy," as one leading Biafran once told me, for a *confederal solution* ever since October 1967—that is over sixteen months ago—when Mr. Arnold Smith of the Commonwealth Secretariat began very actively to urge both sides for a compromise solution.

My principal argument had been that the war was already costing and was likely to continue to cost much more in lives than most of us anticipated or considered reasonable, and that any arrangement which stopped the conflict and the killings quickly while at the same time securing for the Biafrans their *security* and greater local autonomy would satisfy their basic needs. I stressed the point that many more African heads of state would come out to support a middle-of-the-road solution that guaranteed Biafra's basic needs, but did not violate Nigeria's territorial integrity. The clear reserve, and in some quarters hostility, with which African countries still treated the idea of secession despite the sympathy which the Ibo massacres of 1966 had aroused in them, began increasingly to reinforce whatever initial doubts some of us privately harboured as to whether outright secession was in fact the most effective and realistic answer to our problem. I was definitely opposed to surrender. But I was equally anxious for an honourable end to the war. When full scale talks eventually took place first in Kampala and later in Addis Ababa, Lagos repeatedly put forward their conditions for a cease-fire and settlement—renunciation of secession and the acceptance of the twelve-state formula. For me, having at last got Lagos to the conference table, both occasions were our opportunities to reject the twelve-state formula and to make positive proposals for an *Aburi style confederal formula*. On both occasions we failed to be positive. We only insisted on a ceasefire. How realistic is it to hope to obtain a meaningful cease-fire from an opponent who was at that time militarily at an advantage without any reliable hint, even through trusted third parties, that we were prepared in exchange for their stopping the war to reconsider at least the question of sovereignty? At this point I became convinced that our leadership was bent on formal sovereignty much more than I considered reasonable. For me this was a most dangerous game in view of the large stakes involved.

I had never believed that prevarications aimed at trying to trick the opponent would work. The issues involved were basic and ultimate answers to them had to be direct. We were in a hurry.

The mass of our people were already in sufficient danger and anyone causing unnecessary delay to a quick and honourable end to their sufferings was doing them gross disservice. As weeks passed and my frustration increased I began to find it more and more difficult to suppress what I thought and believed. I spoke freely with leading Biafrans on this subject. I got the unmistakable impression that many of them were prepared, if only to put an end to the mounting deaths among the civilians, to accept a *confederal solution* based largely on the *Aburi accord*.

Needless to say, my criticism of the official *hard* line produced several internal clashes. Having carefully reviewed and reflected on the long chain of developments and my disagreements with the leadership's handling of many important issues in this conflict, and finding myself unable to escape the painful conclusion that the difference which divided us as far as the ultimate goal was concerned (for me that goal was and still is real and adequate security for the lives and property of Biafrans) was a fundamental one, in September 1968 I addressed an official communication to the Permanent Secretary, Ministry of Foreign Affairs, formally setting out my views. After some three months of further reflection and finding that my views had undergone no change, I formally tendered my letter of resignation (December 1968), in which I made it clear that the only serious point at issue was the government's attitude toward a negotiated settlement. I do not believe that there is any point in negotiating at all if neither side is prepared for real compromise. Biafra has two things at stake at any talks—*sovereignty* and *security*. I consider it realistic in our present circumstances to think seriously in terms of agreeing to merge this new and as yet shaky sovereignty with that of the rest of Nigeria, but to insist in exchange for this offer on an arrangement which like the *Aburi accord* guarantees for Biafra adequate control of her security.

What became very clear to me in retrospect and rather late is that although most of us gave spontaneous support to the Ibo cause in its broad outline, principally as a reaction against the inexplicable massacres of Ibos in September-October 1966, the only thing that we all had in common was that we were moving in one direction. Our exact destinations were not the same. This fact was not clear at the beginning but as we progressed along the path the divergence of aims and ambitions became increasingly apparent.

As an Ibo from the Mid-Western Region, I had every technical excuse to keep out of a quarrel between the Federal Government and the Eastern Regional Government. I joined the struggle on the Eastern Nigerian side when I did because I was convinced that the Federal Military Government had failed to give the Ibos the protection and care that was their right. I am still convinced that the Ibos have not got this right and will continue to support or fight for any realistic move to secure it for them. What I disagree with is to gamble with the Ibos and Ibo misfortune for uncertain political stakes. This I did oppose quietly and strictly internally for some fourteen months to no avail. As will be seen in the body of the book, I am equally opposed to the extreme and rigid position of the Federal Government. It was reckless extremism in politics during the civilian days that wrecked what was Nigeria and ultimately led to the present bloody confusion. The same recklessness and extremism in military conflict is now threatening to destroy the best hopes of sane people on either side.

If innocent and largely ignorant people die because of faulty decisions which we take on their behalf, the minimum expected of those of us alive who are privileged to know what is happening is to speak out against this reckless and costly extremism. We have been at this bloody game for the past twenty months. We have seen enough during this period to make it clear that however justified our original intentions and objectives may have been, a lot is going seriously wrong. Whether the war is one of *genocide* as Biafra puts it or is merely a *police action* as Lagos once claimed, what matters right now is to find a way of stopping it honourably for both sides. Anyone, no matter on which side he is, who is in a position to do this but prefers to prolong it, is doing so for reasons that cannot conceivably be in the interest of the civilian masses, whose current plight speaks for itself, nor of the young soldiers being sent to early and unnecessary deaths.

Raph Uwechue.

Paris
March 1969.

ACKNOWLEDGEMENTS

For this little production I have an enormous amount of acknowledgement of assistance to make. My thanks go first of all to both President Léopold Sédar Senghor and ex-President Nnamdi Azikiwe for considering it worthwhile to write, each in his own way, so flattering a foreword to this humble work.

Next comes Mr. René Benezra, whose friendship came with our first contact in May 1966, only two days after my arrival to open Nigeria's Embassy in Paris. His fatherly encouragement and unswerving attachment to a sense of fair play regarding this protracted crisis helped me to sustain my convictions and my will to act in accordance with them. But for him the idea of this book would never have matured.

My thanks go also to Mr. Edouard Pelissier and his daughter Dominique, the former for allowing me the use of his personal library, the latter for associating herself with the translation of the text into French.

To Dr. Aloysius Ogwu for reading the manuscript and making many useful and concrete suggestions.

To Chukwuji G. Ashibuogwu for his invaluable contribution regarding the structure of the proposed six states and for drawing all the maps contained in this book.

To Si Bechir Ben Yahmed and Mr. Justin Vieyra, Director and Editor-in-Chief of *Jeune Afrique* respectively, for the enthusiasm and interest with which they urged the speedy publication of the book.

To Mr. Walter Schwarz for assistance not only in granting me his kind permission to quote extensively from his new book *Nigeria* with regard to the confused events of January 1966, but also for useful contribution to the development of my thoughts especially in connection with the chapter on secession.

To Mrs. Katy Brooks for many useful suggestions regarding the text and style of the new edition.

My most sincere thanks go unreservedly to Miss Hélène Berthou, for devoting innumerable leisure hours to typing and retyping the entire manuscript written in one of the world's worst handwritings.

Finally I will wish to record my total indebtedness to my wife Austa whose steady and devoted encouragement throughout the present crisis formed the basis of my determination to go ahead with this work.

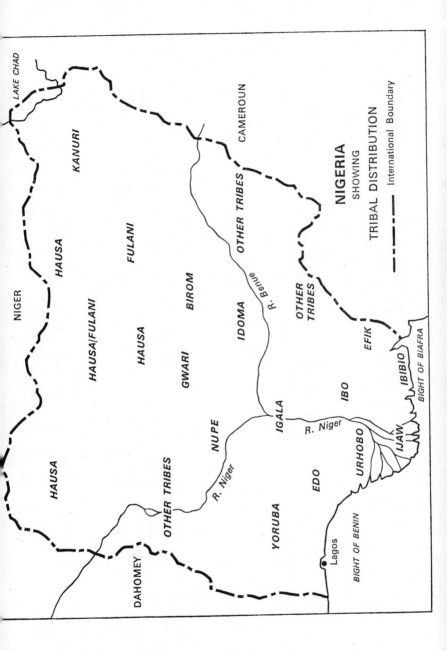

NIGERIA

SHOWING

TRIBAL DISTRIBUTION

–·–·– International Boundary

NIGERIA

SHOWING

THE REGIONS BEFORE MAY 1967

International Boundary

Regional Boundary

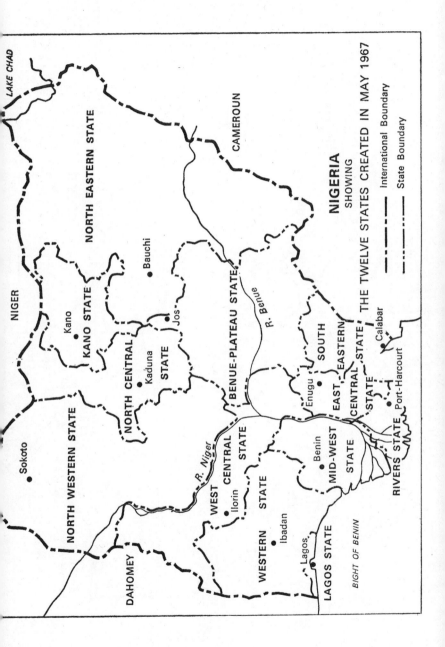

NIGERIA

SHOWING

THE TWELVE STATES CREATED IN MAY 1967

International Boundary

State Boundary

NIGERIA
SHOWING
SIX STATES PROPOSAL
— · — · — International Boundary
State Boundary

REFLECTIONS
ON THE
NIGERIAN CIVIL WAR

Facing the Future

BACKGROUND INFORMATION
ON NIGERIA

History and Constitutional Development

As far back as the tenth century, the great caravan trade routes across the Sahara established contact between the people of what later became Northern Nigeria and the states of North Africa.

From this early period began the intermingling of religious, economic and intellectual influences much of which is today reflected in the life of Nigeria. It is from this period too that much of the early history of Nigeria has been recorded. In Southern Nigeria, the first contact with Europe was in 1486, when the Portuguese visited the Bight of Benin and penetrated inland into the heart of the ancient kingdom of Benin. The English arrived in 1539. Early in the nineteenth century, a Jihad (Islamic religious war) under the great Fulani leader Usuman Dan Fodio swept across the Northern parts of Nigeria and Dan Fodio's lieutenants were as a result established as Emirs in the areas he conquered. Today we find their descendants as the traditional rulers of Northern Nigeria, except in Bornu where the Kanuris effectively resisted and finally expelled the Fulani invaders.

In the eighteenth century trade in commodities gave way to the slave trade and it was in part for the suppression of the latter that the first British Consulate was established at Calabar in 1851 and Lagos was occupied in 1861. In 1885, the year in which the Berlin Conference partitioned Africa, according to Britain exclusive influence over what is now Nigeria, the Oil Rivers Protec-

3

torate covering the Niger Delta area and its immediate vicinity was created. But it was not until the Niger Coast Protectorate including the whole of the southern part of Nigeria came into being in 1893 that there was any real effort at government. Before then the administration of the Niger and Benue valleys was in the hands of the Royal Niger Company, an amalgam of several British trading interests in those parts and under a Royal Charter.

On 1st January 1900, the Royal Niger Company's charter was revoked and the administration of the territory was formally taken over by the British government. In 1906, the Colony and Protectorate of Lagos became part of Southern Nigeria. At the same time a protectorate was established over Northern Nigeria.

On 1st January 1914, the two Protectorates were merged with Lagos into the Colony and Protectorate of Nigeria with Sir Frederick Lugard as Governor-General. The constitutional arrangement introduced at this time provided for two lieutenant governors directly under the Governor-General. The one who administered the Southern Sector had a Legislative Council, to which Nigerians were nominated, to advise him but the governor of the Northern Provinces ruled his own area without an equivalent advisory body. This council was enlarged in 1922 to permit greater Nigerian representation. At this date also the mandated territory of the British Cameroons was attached to Nigeria for administrative purposes.

In 1946 the Richards Constitution—so called after the then Governor of Nigeria Sir Arthur Richards—introduced a federal pattern of government. Under it a central legislature sitting in the federal capital Lagos, was set up to administer the whole country and regional houses of assembly were established in the regional capitals of Enugu (East), Ibadan (West), and Kaduna (North) to act as advisory bodies to the central legislature on regional matters. (The Mid-West Region with Benin as its capital was a later arrival, having been excised from the Western Region only in 1962.) A further revision of the constitution was carried out in 1951 to give greatly increased regional autonomy, larger and more representative legislatures with wide powers both in the regions and at the centre, and to give Nigerians a fuller share in the shaping of government policy and the direction of executive action. The constitution was again revised in 1954. The new constitution gave increased powers to the regions and established the Southern Cameroons (then a part of Nigeria) as a quasi-federal territory. Lagos was declared a federal territory and became administratively separated from the Western Region. The House of Representatives was enlarged to allow each administrative division in Nigeria to be represented by at least one member.

Further constitutional talks were held in London in May and June of 1957 as a result of which the Federal Council of Ministers was constituted on the basis of an all-Nigerian body except for the British Governor-General, who continued to act as president of the Council. The first Federal Prime Minister, in the person of Sir Abubakar Tafawa Balewa, was appointed in August 1957. Regional self-government was given to Eastern and Western Nigeria at the same time. Regional self-government which was delayed at the request of its leaders came to Northern Nigeria two years later in March 1959.

On 1st October 1960, Nigeria became an independent state within the British Commonwealth with the Queen as the titular Head of State. Three years later, on 1st October 1963, she became a republic still within the Commonwealth but with a Nigerian President in the person of Dr. Nnamdi Azikiwe as Head of State.

The Republican Constitution as it then stood came to an abrupt end on 15th January 1966. Prolonged political disturbances were climaxed by a bloody coup d'etat (carried out by a few young military officers and in which the country's Prime Minister Sir Abubakar Tafawa Balewa was killed), and the Nigerian Armed Forces—army, navy and police—were formally invited by the remnant of the civilian government to take over the administra-

5

tion of the country. Major General Aguiyi-Ironsi, the then head of the Nigerian army, became the head of the Federal Military Government. On 24th May 1966 he promulgated the Decree No. 34 which set aside the regional arrangement in preference to a unitary system. Both General Ironsi and his decree succumbed two months later when another military coup in which he perished removed him from office and promptly revoked the offending decree. Nigeria now under a new military leader, Lt. Col. Yakubu Gowon, thus reverted to the federal system.

Following continued civil and military disturbances involving large scale massacres, the movement of population—with all its implications of social and economic dislocation—and fierce political disagreements among the military leaders themselves, it became clear that a new constitutional formula, which would take into practical account the changes that had occurred, was urgently needed. An Ad Hoc Constitutional Conference with representatives from the four regions and Lagos was convened in mid-September 1966 to try to find a solution to the existing constitutional and administrative chaos. It died in the cradle choked by an atmosphere heavily laden with distrust and bitterness. After abortive attempts to meet locally, Nigerian military leaders went to Aburi (Ghana) in January 1967 and under the chairmanship of Lt. General Ankrah, then chairman of Ghana's Liberation Committee, decided on important changes in the constitution. In spite of heated disagreement between the Federal Military Government on the one hand and the East Regional Military Government on the other as to the details of what was agreed, it is nevertheless clear both from the printed verbatim report and from the tape-recorded account of the proceedings of the conference, that basically there was agreement to introduce a greater measure of decentralization by increasing the powers of the regions vis-à-vis those of the Federal Government.*

* See Appendix A for a record of agreements reached at Aburi.

Endless haggling over the *Aburi accord* led to mounting tension and the constitutional explosion came when, as a move to forestall the threatened breakaway of the Eastern Region, the Federal Military Government suddenly split the country into twelve states and thus precipitated the secession of the Eastern Region only three days afterwards on 30th May 1967. Lt. Col. Odumegwu Ojukwu, the Military Governor of the East, named his new state Biafra and assumed the post of Head of State. The Federal Military Government refused to recognize the Eastern Region's right to secession, declaring the act of a rebellion.

The War

On 6th July 1967, the Federal Government launched what was then described as a "police action" intended to discipline "Lt. Col. Ojukwu and his clique." The campaign was expected to last a few weeks or a few months at the most.

The federal army, which only the previous July numbered less than nine thousand men, had multiplied in the interval to an estimated forty thousand troops, hurriedly reconstructed from the disorganized remnants of the Nigerian army after the withdrawal of eastern Nigerian elements. It had acquired a few dozen British armoured vehicles of the Ferret and Saladin type as well as a number of French Panhards. The absence of Ibo officers— who formed the bulk of the officer class in the old Nigerian army —meant that the new federal army had to rely mainly on inexperienced young officers or on more seasoned but uneducated non-commissioned officers. This lacuna prompted widespread speculation in the early days of the war that foreign mercenaries were leading the federal troops. It is not clear how much truth there was in this allegation but there is little doubt that the engineering corps made excessive use of foreign "instructors."

The Biafran army at the beginning of the war was estimated at some twenty-five thousand troops hurriedly organized around the nucleus of the two thousand surviving Eastern Nigerian officers and men. What little training there was took place in secret makeshift camps. The bulk of recruitment came initially from the abundant supply of angry refugee youths itching for the opportunity to fight. The Biafran army was relatively lightly armed, relying on clandestine shipments of weapons many of which came initially from Czechoslovakia. It had no artillery and very few anti-tank weapons. Nevertheless, Biafran morale, spurred by the burning desire to avenge themselves for the 1966 massacres, was very high.

There was no real air force on either side. The federal air force only just created consisted of a bare dozen trainer aircrafts of the Dornier type. Biafra had two American-built B-26 bombers purchased clandestinely in France. She also had a number of French-built helicopters originally bought as civilian machines by companies operating in the Eastern Region.

The federal army opened its campaign by advancing from the North with a reported strength of eight battalions. The Biafrans had expected the advance from that direction and had taken positions weeks before that event. Biafran resistance was much stiffer than expected. Although increased federal pressure led to the loss in the first weeks of fighting of important portions of Ogoja province, the Biafrans took a heavy toll of the federal army.

On 9th August 1967, Biafran forces in a lightning operation overran the Mid-West state and within the next few days advanced some thirty miles into the heart of Nigeria's Western Region. This event and the shock it produced, perhaps more than any other factor, fundamentally altered the character of the war. That unexpected push revealed in a dramatic fashion Biafran military capabilities. Lagos itself came under very real threat. This fact induced a rapid re-thinking on the federal side: "From now on," General Gowon declared, "we shall wage a total war."

This decision led directly to the involvement of the big powers on the Nigerian side, for Lagos made quick and decisive use of its international status to seek foreign aid. Britain and Russia obliged —the former because she wanted to retain her privileged place in Nigeria, while the latter saw a golden opportunity to obtain a foothold in West Africa.

The support of these two powers for the Federal Government made all the difference in the war. From Britain, federal land forces received ample supplies of light and heavy weapons. The federal air force was entirely reorganized and equipped with Russian Mig fighters and Ilyushin bombers. "Total war" became a reality. In late September 1967, the Biafran forces were swept back from the Mid-West into the Eastern Region. A fortnight later the Biafran capital of Enugu fell into federal hands. By the end of the year Biafra's second largest port of Calabar also went. The important river port and commercial centre, Onitsha, fell. Port-Harcourt was to follow in May 1968, thus making the blockade of Biafra total. The subsequent fall of the remaining big towns of Aba, Umuahia and Owerri in quick succession spoke more of superior federal military might than of higher federal morale or better fighting methods.

The "total war" and the enormity of civilian suffering which it produced attracted increasing world attention and sympathy for the Biafrans. This development led directly to the recognition of Biafra by four African states—Tanzania (13 April 1968), Gabon (8 May 1968), Ivory Coast (14 May 1968), and Zambia (20 May 1968). Their decision was prompted largely by the failure of the Federal Military Government to respond to appeals to settle the conflict otherwise than by force of arms. Duvalier's Haiti gave Biafra official recognition (23 March 1969), but not for the same reasons.

International recognition for Biafra provoked unexpected counterreactions. It encouraged the hawks on the Biafran side to intransigence as far as peace negotiations were concerned. An infuriated Federal Government decided that more force was the answer. For Biafra recognition brought increased material support. In addition to vital transit facilities it enjoyed in Lisbon and in Portuguese African territories, French arms slipped in steadily through Abidjan and Libreville. This skeleton supply coupled with the morale of the Biafran population frustrated successive federal "final offensives," postponing the end of the war till January 1970.

Indirect support for the Biafran government came from several charitable organizations. Basically concerned with the plight of the civilian population, these organizations—the International Red Cross, Joint Church Aid, Caritas, and a number of national Red Cross organizations—ignored the political and legalistic sophistry by which both sides tried to put military considerations before those of relief. Mutual suspicion killed the chances of relief by sea and land routes. General Ojukwu persistently refused daylight relief flights into Biafra without an effective third party guarantee that Lagos would not use such flights to military advantage. He preferred night flights—which Lagos opposed but could not effectively check—that gave his gunrunning aircrafts ideal cover. Federal disenchantment with the backing Biafra received from relief organizations increased with the length of the war. The climax came in June 1969 when federal Migs shot down an International Red Cross relief plane killing its crew of four. Henceforth the organization became passively "neutral," suspending its activities in the absence of agreement between Ojukwu and Lagos. The other organizations, led by Joint Church Aid and Caritas, consistently ignored federal disapproval. At war's end the different policies paid off differently. The International Red Cross was reinstated by the victorious Federal Government. The "offending" relief organizations were asked to withdraw.

Peace Talks

Anxious to avoid appearing to encourage the principle of secession, the O.A.U. (Organization for African Unity) stuck rigidly throughout the war to the principle of settlement "within the context of one Nigeria." At its summit meeting in Kinshasa (September 1967) it made only a timid attempt to intervene in the conflict. It appointed a Consultative Peace Committee of six, headed by Emperor Haile Selassie, to examine the issue. Initially, very little came from that committee. African aversion to secession came largely from fears that any Biafran success would trigger off similar movements in an explosive continent, practically all of whose countries are recent creations with artificial boundaries. There were also those Africans who opposed secession because in Nigeria's immense potential they saw Africa's earliest hope for the emergence of a powerful and prestigious modern state.

In October 1967 Mr. Arnold Smith, the Commonwealth Secretary-General, sought to open negotiations with a view to finding a compromise solution. A preliminary confrontation took place in London in April 1968. This meeting succeeded in accepting the principle of settlement by negotiation. As Biafra objected to holding full-scale talks in London, which it regarded as hostile territory on the grounds that the British government was backing Lagos, Kampala was selected as a neutral venue.

The delegates assembled in the Ugandan capital in May 1968. The Lagos delegation was headed by Chief Anthony Enahoro, Nigeria's Commissioner for Information. The Biafrans were led by Sir Louis Mbanefo, their Chief Justice. Biafran objections to the "preponderance of British influence" in the Commonwealth Secretariat led to a demand that the talks should be presided over by President Obote himself, who had the dual attribute of being a Commonwealth and an African head of state. Finally, agreement was reached for a joint chairmanship of the Commonwealth Secretary-General and the Ugandan Foreign Minister.

Lagos laid down its conditions for a cease-fire and settlement—renunciation of secession and acceptance of its twelve-state formula. The Biafran delegation countered with the demand that a cease-fire should precede any full-scale discussions. Within a week the talks broke down. Sir Louis Mbanefo, who was the first to leave Kampala, declared: "We have not come all the way from Biafra simply to sign an act of surrender in distant Kampala." (It is one of the memorable ironies of the civil war that he was later —15 January 1970—at war's end to accompany a delegation to sign an act of unconditional surrender much nearer home, in Lagos.) The Kampala proceedings set an ominous pattern for future peace conferences.

Although it failed, Kampala secured an important by-product. This bold Commonwealth initiative encouraged the dormant O.A.U. Consultative Committee to see things differently. Direct approaches were made to the Biafran leadership, opening the way to a series of peace attempts. On its invitation, General Ojukwu addressed the committee in Niamey, capital of the Niger Republic (July 1968). This move was immediately followed by a "probing" meeting of delegations from both sides, who raised hopes of peaceful settlement by announcing their agreement that full-scale talks would take place the following month in Addis Ababa. Generals Gowon and Ojukwu were widely expected to lead their respective delegations. However, when the representatives assembled in the first week of August 1968, in the Ethiopian capital, only General Ojukwu was there. Within days the talks collapsed. Eight months later (April 1969), another abortive attempt was made in Monrovia. General Gowon was engaged on a more important issue—celebrating his marriage. General Ojukwu was unavailable for other important reasons. A similar fate met a further attempt at Addis Ababa in mid-December 1969. This fifth attempt proved the last.

One thing that emerged clearly from these abortive experiments was the fact that the basic issue on which settlement itself revolved was consistently circumvented. Both sides repeatedly proclaimed their readiness to negotiate "without preconditions" but attached different interpretations to this term. For Lagos, it meant negotiating in accordance with the O.A.U. resolution aimed at preserving Nigeria's territorial integrity. For Biafra it meant respecting the status quo which by implication involved a *de facto* acceptance of her sovereignty. The Federal Military Government continuously stressed the conflict's juridical aspect involving Nigeria's territorial integrity, speaking only in vague terms on the question of security which was uppermost in the minds of millions of Biafrans. Too avid for the conventional trappings of formal sovereignty, the Biafran leadership remained studiously—and, as events later proved, foolishly—mute on concrete proposals concerning possible security arrangements within an eventual Nigerian federation.

In January 1970 the stalemate was brutally and decisively resolved. Exhaustion from a long blockade and newly acquired Russian armaments smashed both Biafran morale and defences. First Owerri, the provisional capital and last major town in Biafran hands, then the lone airport of Uli fell within days of each other. On 8th January 1970, General Ojukwu fled Biafra. Four days later, his successor—Major General Effiong—sued for peace. On 15th January 1970, at General Gowon's Dodan barracks, he signed the formal act of surrender, with the following unequivocal declaration: "We accept the existing administrative and political structure of the federation of Nigeria. Biafra ceases to exist."

The collapse of Biafra put an end to the military aspect of the Nigerian drama. But the end of the war has not removed the cause of a conflict born of long-standing political problems, the most acute among which was the question of security for the Ibos within the Nigerian federation. This socio-political problem remains to be solved. It is on the type of solution achieved that depends the political future of Nigeria.

Geography, Peoples and Religion

The Republic of Nigeria, with a surface area of some 400,000 square miles, is on the West Coast of Africa. It lies between latitudes 4° and 14° north of the Equator and longitudes 3° and 14° east. Nigeria's immediate neighbours are the following four French-speaking countries—Dahomey to the West; Niger to the North; Chad to the North-East; and Cameroun to the East.

Although Nigeria lies wholly within the tropics, the climate and vegetation vary from tropical at the coast to sub-tropical in the Northern end of the country. There are two well-marked seasons: wet and dry. The rainy season usually lasts from April to October, and the dry season from November to March. There is an abundance of sunshine and warmth all the year round.

Temperatures at the coast vary from 70° to 90° F, but humidity is fairly uniformly high. In the Northern end, the climate is drier and extremes of temperature are more common from October to April—sometimes reaching as high as 110° F. The lowest temperature is 50° F. Nevertheless, despite these predominating tropical conditions, there are some hill and plateau areas which enjoy a climate not less congenial than those of the temperate regions of the world.

One of Nigeria's characteristic features is its division into three unequal geographical sectors by its two great rivers—the River Niger and its main tributary, the River Benue. The Niger runs through the country from North-West to South, a distance of about 750 miles. The Benue has its source in the Cameroun mountains on Nigeria's North-Eastern border and joins the Niger at Lojoka after a distance of about 500 miles.

Along the coast there are lagoons, creeks and thick mangrove swamps, through which runs an intricate but useful system of inland waterways. Behind this is the forest belt, from 50 to 100 miles in depth, and beyond this lies the Savannah woodland. North of the confluence of the Rivers Niger and Benue is a plateau averaging over 2,000 feet above sea level. In parts of the plateau, there are heights of over 6,000 feet. In the extreme North, the country merges into the Sahara and slopes gently down towards Lake Chad in the North-East.

Nigeria's population of 55 million is the largest on the African continent, well distancing that of the United Arab Republic (30 million), which comes next to it. It comprises some 250 ethnic groups with a variety of customs, traditions, languages and dialects.

The larger groups are as follows: *Hausa, Fulani, Tiv, Kanuri,* and *Nupe* in the Northern parts; the *Yoruba, Edo, Urhobo, Itsekiri* and *Ijaw* in the Western parts; the *Ibo, Ibibio, Efik* and *Ijaw* in the Eastern parts.

Nigeria is thus like many other African states a conglomeration of ethnic groups brought together to form a modern state by the influence and power of former colonial masters.

English is the *lingua franca* but the following are among the most popular of the traditional languages which are not only widely spoken but have their own literature: *Hausa*—predominant in the North; *Yoruba* and *Edo*—predominant in the Western parts; *Ibo* and *Efik*—predominant in the Eastern parts.

Islam is the predominant religion in the Northern part of the country and is also practised but in a much lesser degree in parts of Western Nigeria. The Southern part of the country is mainly Christian and here the various denominations—Catholics, Protestants, Methodists, Presbyterians—exist side by side. Of late, Christianity has made some—though still limited—inroad in parts of Northern Nigeria, especially among the animists of that region. There are also important pockets of animists in Western, Mid-Western and Eastern Nigeria.

A TIME FOR REFLECTION

> The only thing necessary for the triumph of evil is for good men to do nothing.
>
> Edmund Burke

It is now exactly three years and three months since January 1966, when the nation took its first formal step on the path towards the present bloody revolution. That step was taken on her behalf by a handful of young army officers. Since then a great deal has happened. The revolution which those few triggers sparked off has not only consumed most of its originators but is now about to consume the nation itself. This is therefore the moment to pause and think—a time for serious reflection.

At a time such as this when peace moves, which held out so much hope not only for Nigerians and Biafrans alike but indeed for many of their common friends inside and outside Africa, appear clearly to be faltering, partly because of the obstacles created by misguided and short-sighted extremists in both camps, it is my belief that the moment has come to rally men and women of good will on both sides as well as their friends inside and outside Africa to act in time enough to save what is left of the nation and our people.

I have been encouraged to set the ideas that follow on paper for public consumption by certain convictions which I have had

for a long time now—convictions embodied in views I had trie
in vain to preach in private to a limited and, as it turned ou
adamant group. I am doing this in the new hope that a wide
audience will lend perhaps a more favourable ear. These convic
tions may be put down as follows:

1. Following the incidents of 1966 and their consequent expo
sure of the fatal weaknesses of our political system and methods
most people now on either side of the present conflict took
their respective positions because they wished to correct—cer
tainly not to exploit—those weaknesses, in order to achieve greate
security to life and property and to prevent a recurrence of the
gruesome experience of 1966. In other words, what sane and
reasonable people on both sides set out to achieve was not the
destruction of Nigerian and Biafran lives and property but the
very opposite of this—their greater protection and preservation

2. What is now happening is not, in my view, leading to tha
original objective. Indeed, in announcing his government's de
cision to invade the Eastern Region, General Yakubu Gowor
told his supporters that the operation upon which he was em
barking was merely a *police action* intended to soften the resist
ance of Lt. Col. "Ojukwu and his clique," and restore peace and
unity to the country. Whatever may have been his other unspoken
motives for this move, if there were any, there is nevertheless
the extenuating evidence that his original military preparation
was, at the time he launched his attack, aimed at an instrument
considerably short of the present gigantic machine geared for
total war. It did not envisage, for example, a reinvigorated air
force capable of carrying out the atrocious and devastating work
done against the civilian population by his present Russian-built
air force.

Lt. Col. Ojukwu for his part, in the face of the overwhelming
tragedy that befell his people, had told Easterners to come home
to their own region where he hoped to provide for them the

ecurity that had so evidently eluded them in most parts of the ederation since the riots of May 1966. In his hopes to comfort nd reassure his tragedy-stricken charge, Lt. Col. Ojukwu had romised that he would see to their security to the extent that 'No Power In Black Africa" could dare hurt them again.

It was largely this kind of assurance from both leaders—

a) from General Gowon that he planned no large scale destruction of life and property or the extermination of Easterners as a people,

b) from Lt. Col. Ojukwu that he was well prepared for any eventuality and that he was militarily strong enough to offer the required protection to his people in the event of an armed conflict

–that influenced reasonable men and women on either side to give their support to these two young military leaders on the understanding that as soldiers, their professional etiquette and code of honour were adequate guarantees that they would be bound by their words. Few people at the time whether in Nigeria or Biafra contemplated the present holocaust.

What has happened since 6th July 1967, when federal forces began their promised *police action*, and what is still happening are now public knowledge. Events since that date and the course which the struggle has taken do clearly show that the mandate given to the leaders by the people on either side has become not only overstretched but is actually being abused to the detriment of the very people—men, women and especially innocent children —whose welfare and security are and should be their primary concern. By bombing hundreds of civilians to death and destroying the homes and property of hundred of thousands more, the Federal Government can hardly justify its claims to be protecting and liberating the very same people. By doing nothing to discourage and perhaps by positively encouraging through intensive propaganda its own supporters to the baneful notion of "mass suicide if need be," Lt. Col. Ojukwu's government has not put itself in a stronger moral position than that of Lagos.

Anyone who has followed closely the terrible experience undergone by Biafrans—especially the Ibos—during the massacres of 1966, and the equally harrowing experience which has been their lot since the present war began, can neither fail to appreciate the reasons for the progressive hardening of Biafran feelings against the rest of Nigeria, nor to admire the courage and gallantry which the soldier and the ordinary man and woman have shown in this struggle. There is no doubt that after all that has happened, the Biafran people have a just cause to revolt in one form or the other. But if the object in view is to alleviate the effect of this tragedy rather than to worsen it, then it is the duty of responsible leadership to coax and guide a justly embittered people towards the most salutary and beneficial objectives. Without neglecting its obligations to the memory of the dead, Biafran leadership has a more positive and definite responsibility to the living—to see that as many of them as possible go on living. This is—or was—the purpose of the entire struggle. Viewed otherwise it is meaningless. *Sovereignty or mass suicide* is an irresponsible slogan unworthy of the sanction or encouragement of any serious and sensible leadership.

The purpose of the struggle was—and should so remain—to secure for the people the right to a decent life in adequate security. Sovereignty for Biafra should be correctly seen and taken for what it originally was—a means (one out of a number of possible means) to this end. With the situation as it is at present, it is wrong to persist in sacrificing everything including innocent children in an inflexible quest for sovereignty. Nigeria is already a sovereign state.

Today's Biafrans and other Nigerians have basked proudly in the glory and comfort of her sovereignty ever since independence was achieved in 1960.

Remaining in the Nigerian fold and continuing to enjoy the same accustomed sovereignty involves no stigma. Suffice it to say that nearly two years after the proclamation of Biafra's separation from Nigeria, travelling Biafrans like other Nigerians are realistic enough to cling to the protection and privileges accorded them by the Nigerian passport—that is by Nigerian sovereignty. What Biafrans lacked and what produced the present bitter and unfortunate conflict therefore is not sovereignty. *It is security*. It is the duty of the leadership to take the pains and risks involved in bringing home this vital distinction to the masses who, left alone in their present mood of intensive but justified anger, cannot see the difference unaided. It is here that leadership comes in and it is here that it should be judged.

In the light of past and present experience the one absolute necessity—and this is what Biafrans should be prepared, if need be, to fight and die for—is that any settlement must be based on the twin principle of *Nigerian sovereignty cum Biafran security*.

For the ordinary people to die for "sovereignty" which they already possess within Nigeria is madness. For anyone in authority to lead them to do so is to delude them. The correct slogan should be *security or death;* certainly not *sovereignty or death.*

3. While it is normal, even though undesirable, for peoples anywhere in the world to disagree to the extent of engaging in armed conflict, for a people essentially of the same stock to continue to massacre themselves in such numbers—and this with *massive foreign assistance*, and by implication encouragement—to produce no other result than the destruction of their own and their children's long term interests and perhaps, in a wider sense, the destruction of one of Africa's best hopes for a prosperous and possibly glorious future, is a thought provoking tragedy intolerably depressing to any true African or friend of Africa.

4. Military victory for either side whenever it does come, no matter how impressive its temporary success may be, is no basis for a lasting solution of our problem. The matter in question

being essentially a sociological and a political one, can only be resolved by a proper approach to it from this angle. In a family fight involving so much bloodshed and loss of lives, there can be no real winner, as the entire family is the ultimate loser.

5. The above situation being the case, whether as Nigerians or Biafrans the stage has been reached when we have to realize and admit, with no sense of shame, that having missed our way to the desired objective, it has now become our duty to muster the necessary moral courage to reexamine our map with a view to retracing our way a few steps in order to seek the correct road to our intended destination.

As Lt. Col. Odumegwu Ojukwu himself aptly summarized our present unfortunate plight in his marathon address to the O.A.U. Consultative Committee in Addis Ababa on the fifth of August 1968, "This has been not only a most brutal and ruinous but a most senseless and fruitless war." There is evidence that his chief adversary and one-time friend and comrade-in-arms, General Yakubu Gowon holds a similar view. If this were the case, why then do we continue to prosecute so "senseless and fruitless" a war? I believe that this tragic anomaly reveals the absence of an all-important factor—the lack of positive action on the part of millions of Nigerians and Biafrans who share this same view. How much sacrifice have we been able to make; how much punishment have we dutifully absorbed in order to kill ourselves and destroy our property? The effort involved in a more realistic and constructive approach does not even call for so much sacrifice. Why then should we in our right senses continue to prefer the destructive and more arduous alternative? Nigerians and Biafrans, wake up and think. Now is the time to do so.

CHAPTER 2

THE REVOLUTION OF JANUARY 1966— MISMANAGED AND MISUNDERSTOOD

Several accounts have been published of the events of January 1966. Many of these are contradictory in important details. Bearing in mind the time through which we are passing this is hardly surprising.

Being myself an Ibo and thus coming from that ethnic group which has been collectively accused of conspiracy to plot and perpetrate the military coup d'etat of January 1966, I have solicited and obtained, for the purpose of greater objectivity, the kind permission of Mr. Walter Schwarz, author of the recent book *Nigeria*, to quote in full his account of the fateful events of January 1966 as seen by an outsider—a non-Ibo and a non-Nigerian.

Lagos (Federal Capital)

On the night of January 14-15 a big party was given in the Lagos home of Brigadier Maimalari, the North's senior army Officer. Soon after it broke up, truckloads of soldiers from Abeokuta barracks, between Lagos and Ibadan in the Western Region, moved into Lagos. A detachment led by Major Emanuel Ifeajuna arrested the Federal Prime Minister in his house. Balewa left quietly after saying his prayers. The same group also took away Chief Festus Okotie-Eboh, the wealthy and influential Minister of Finance, from his house next door. Chief Festus was reported to have struggled violently and to have been beaten. The power station, telephone exchange, cable and broadcasting station were put under guard. The three most senior Northern officers, Brigadier Maimalari, Lt. Col. Pam (Adjudant-General) and Lt. Col. Largema (Commander, Fourth Battalion), were shot dead: Maimalari and Pam in their homes, Largema at the Ikoyi Hotel where he was staying. Pam, a dashing commander in both the Congo and Tiv operations, and Maimalari had been popular officers throughout the army. There was also an Ibo casualty that night—Lt. Col. Unegbe. He was in charge of the ammunition store at Ikeja barracks and had refused to hand over the keys when asked for them. He, too, was shot dead . . .

Ironsi seemed also to have been intended to die that night. He was at the Maimalari party and later went to another party aboard the Elder Dempster mailboat Aureol at Apapa. When he reached home his telephone was ringing. It was Lt. Col. Pam, who warned him that something was happening, only minutes before Pam himself was shot. Ironsi acted quickly. He drove out of Lagos to the Ikeja garrison. On the way his Landrover was stopped at a rebel checkpoint, but he mustered enough personal authority ("get out of my way") to get through. At Ikeja, Ironsi, who had risen through the ranks, made straight for the regimental sergeant-major's quarters and rallied the garrison. The coup had been foiled and the leaders, Major D. Okafor, head of the Federal Guards, and Major Ifeajuna, fled from the town. According to another version they left for Enugu to effect the coup there, having inadvertently failed to leave reliable officers in charge in Lagos. The bodies of the Prime Minister and the Finance Minister were found a week later in bushes beside the Lagos-Abeokuta road.

Ibadan (Western Region)

At the heavily-guarded Premier's lodge, the soldiers met only token resistance from the police, but inside they met a hail of automatic rifle fire from Akintola himself. In a twenty-five minute exchange the Premier killed several soldiers before finally being taken to their car, . . . Akintola was already badly wounded and he was finished off before his body was bundled into the car . . .

Kaduna (Northern Region)

In Kaduna Major Nzeogwu, the brilliant young chief instructor at the Nigerian Defence Academy, left the Academy early that evening with a detachment of soldiers, mostly Hausa, on "routine exercises." Nzeogwu was an Ibo, from the Mid-West, but he had lived most of his life in the North and spoke better Hausa than Ibo. When his troops were well outside the town, he told them of the real assignment. "They were armed and I was not," he explained later. "They could have shot me if they wished." At the Premier's Lodge three security guards were shot dead and one of the attacking soldiers was killed before the group could enter the grounds. The house was shelled with mortar fire and to get inside Nzeogwu blew the door open with a grenade, injuring his hand. The Sardauna was shot dead, together with one of his wives and two house servants. Meanwhile another group had entered the house of Brigadier Ademulegun, the Yoruba commander of the First Brigade, and shot both him and his wife in bed. Col. Shodeinde, second-in-command at the Defence Academy, also a Yoruba, was shot too; his wife escaped by feigning death at his side.

The North was the only region where the coup went off as planned. On the afternoon of January 15, Nzeogwu broadcast a proclamation "in the name of the Supreme Council of the Revolution," declaring martial law over an area designated for the first time as the "Northern Province of Nigeria." Nzeogwu announced that the constitution was suspended, the regional government and assembly were dissolved, and departments were to be run by their permanent secretaries for the time being. In ten proclamations the death penalty was prescribed for looting, arson, homosexuality and rape, embezzlement, bribery or corruption, obstructing of the revolution, sabotage, subversion, false alarm and assistance to foreign invaders. Nzeogwu went on: "our enemies are the political profiteers, swindlers, the men in high and low places that seek bribes and demand ten percent, those that seek to keep the country permanently divided so that they can remain in office as Ministers and VIPS of waste, the tribalists, the nepotists, those that make the country look big for nothing before international circles." He ended "thank you very much and good-bye for now."

Enugu (Eastern Region)

In Enugu the revolt was short-lived. Soldiers surrounded the Premier's Lodge at 2 A.M. They invested the radio station and the Governor's Lodge, where Archbishop Makarios of Cyprus was staying the night on the last leg of a tour of the Federation. Early listeners to Radio Enugu heard the voice of a studio engineer at 6:30 A.M.: "This is Efiong Etu. The army are here with us in the studio and they have ordered us to tune in to NBC Lagos." At 10 A.M., the Premier, Michael Okpara, and the Governor, Sir Francis Ibiam, were allowed to drive in procession to the airport with the Archbishop and see him off. Soldiers formed a discreet part of the procession. However, Okpara and the other politicians were later allowed to leave Enugu for their home towns and villages. At 2 P.M., on orders from Lagos, soldiers returned to barracks. The failure of the coup in Lagos had scotched the one in Enugu. Whether the presence of Archbishop Makarios had saved Okpara's life, or whether Ibo soldiers had, after all, found it impossible to kill one of their own tribesmen, is not yet clear.

Benin (Midwestern Region)

In the Mid-West capital of Benin, nothing happened until 10 A.M. on January 15. Troops arrived in a detachment from Enugu and surrounded the Premier's and Governor's houses. They were withdrawn, on orders from Lagos, at 2 P.M.

Lagos (January 15th)

At midday a statement broadcast from Lagos said that certain sections of the army had revolted and kidnapped the Prime Minister and the Minister of Finance, but that the "vast majority" of the army remained loyal and that General Ironsi was bringing the situation under control. The General spent the morning at police headquarters trying to live up to this promise. As he emerged a reporter asked him how things were going. "Very badly, indeed," he replied. The army was in a critical condition. A column of troops under Nzeogwu was driving southwards from Kaduna, apparently intending to join other rebel forces in a march on Lagos. They reached Jebba, on the Niger River. Had they crossed, nothing could have stopped them from reaching Ibadan, where troops were already defensively dug in on the Northern approaches. Nigeria seemed close to civil war . . .

Major Nzeogwu did not hold out. A safe-conduct agreement was reached and he returned to Lagos. However, he and the other coup leaders were detained. Ifeajuna had fled, first to Enugu and then to Ghana, but he was persuaded to come back and also was detained.[1]

The intentions and motivations of the young idealists in military uniform who set the current military revolution in motion, on the night of 15th January 1966, have since been a subject of controversy. They are bound to remain so for as long as the present commotion lasts and the temper of the nation remains charged, as at present, with deep and conflicting emotions. For accurate assessment and therefore for fair judgment, both the act itself and the motives behind it will have to wait the historian's post-mortem. At the moment many facts are yet unknown and those that have emerged, being still in the grip of fierce and bitter politics, are inescapably subject to biased political treatment.

However, judging from what evidence has emerged and from such illuminating pointers as, for example, the character and background of perhaps its most prominent organizer and perpetrator, Major Patrick Chukwuma Kaduna Nzeogwu, the intentions of the young men of the January coup were most probably national.

He was a young man whose upbringing and background were calculated to render him blind to tribe and tribal affiliation. He was born in Kaduna (capital of Northern Nigeria)—a fact which explains the origin of one of his first names, Kaduna. Here his parents lived without break for some thirty-four years until they had to flee southwards after the anti-Ibo riots of May 1966. Here in the heart of the North young Kaduna grew up and attended both primary and secondary schools in a totally cosmopolitan atmosphere. (Patrick Chukwuma Nzeogwu attended St. John's

College Kaduna, where I first met him and spent five years with him.) Indeed, it has been said by those who know him well and who kept in close touch with him to his last days, that, although he was with the Biafran army, he fought and died a true and constant son of Nigeria—fighting for what he believed was a conflict to reshape and strengthen Nigeria, not to break or destroy it.

Indeed, while there are hardly any cogent reasons to make the intentions of these young men appear otherwise, there are, on the contrary, many self-evident ones to support the view that they were national. As Walter Schwarz put it very succinctly in his book *Nigeria*, although the coup was "Ibo led" it was nationally inspired.

The endemic and unsavoury political squabbles that characterized the political power play in the six years of Nigeria's independence had the following landmarks, pointing unmistakably to the difficult terrain that lay ahead. These were:

a) the census rumpus of 1962-63 which shook the nation and sowed seeds of distrust in our body politic;

b) the seriously disputed elections to the Federal House of Representatives in 1964, which brought the country to the verge of anarchy and disintegration;

c) the reappearance at the end of 1965 (October-December), in a practically naked form, of an improved version of the same political chicanery that had bedeviled the 1964 federal elections, and Chief Samuel Akintola's consequent attempt in collaboration with Sir Abubakar Tafawa Balewa's Federal Government, to impose through brutal suppression his unpopular clique on the embittered electorate of Western Nigeria.

All these successive events had produced in the minds of many serious-thinking Nigerians a revulsion against the existing kind of politicking, as well as the feeling that the time had come to put at least some form of check on the blatant excesses of a power-drunk and considerably corrupt political breed. It was most probably this important consideration, so widely and so genuinely shared by most educated and even many uneducated Nigerians at the time, that was the prime motive behind the thoughts and action of these young officers, most of them in their middle and late twenties—an ideal age for idealism.

Having as objective to sack the governments of the day and clean up the society, it would appear that in the act of actual execution many things went wrong. Many liberal-minded Nigerians, who saw the situation from a national angle, did manifest clearly their disposition to welcome a change, although they were at the same time gravely dismayed by the fact that blood had to be shed in accomplishing the change. That is to say, while agreeing with the objective they nevertheless bitterly regretted the bloody aspect of the method chosen for its attainment.

In many non-Ibo hearts, the one-sided pattern of killing aroused suspicion that perhaps the coup was an attempt by Ibos to seize power in the country. Given the sectionally-oriented background of our politics, it was difficult for those whose interest suffered as a result of the coup to stop to reflect on the following facts:

a) The coup was indisputably carried out by officers and men of mixed ethnic origins even if the more prominent ones were Ibos.

b) Although the killings in the army affected mainly Western and Northern senior officers, a senior Ibo officer, Lt. Col. Arthur Unegbe, then quartermaster general of the Nigerian Armed Forces, was shot by the young officers precisely for his refusal to cooperate with them.

c) This very act on Lt. Col. Unegbe's part, of giving his life rather than surrender the key of the armory as demanded by the young officers, played a very important part in bringing about the collapse of the coup in Lagos itself. Unable to secure the armory, the leaders of the coup were automatically denied control of the most important means of carrying out their plan in the Lagos area—arms and ammunition. It was, indeed, exactly this situation that gave General Ironsi his chance on that fateful night of 15th January. The loyal troops he rallied at dawn had arms and ammunition to support him.

d) Although they did not suffer the same fate as Lt. Col. Arthur Unegbe, most of the senior Ibo army officers were unaware of the plan to overthrow the government. Here it may be helpful perhaps to mention the fact that Lt. Col. Odumegwu Ojukwu, who was then in charge of the 5th battalion of the Nigerian army stationed in Kano, played a decisive role in ensuring the collapse of the coup. He refused to cooperate with Major Nzeogwu who was then in Kaduna and instead gave his support to General Ironsi in the latter's opposition to the *January Boys*. A grateful Ironsi soon afterwards appointed him Military Governor of Eastern Nigeria.

Indeed, because of the attitude of strong disapproval adopted by Lt. Col. Ojukwu to the January episode, his relations with Major Chukwuma Nzeogwu were strained to such a degree, and the distrust between them so great, that even up to the outbreak of the war some eighteen months after the January event, Major Nzeogwu, despite his undisputed military prowess and near-idolatry popularity with the troops, was not trusted enough by Lt. Col. Ojukwu to be given any command in the new Biafran army.

Such was the extent of opposition harboured by high ranking Ibo army officers to the "Ibo camp" of January 1966.

Nevertheless, in spite of the evidence above, the depth of mis-understanding has been such that there are still today Nigerians who find it impossible to believe that practically all senior officers including General Ironsi had nothing to do with the January plot. According to them, General Ironsi should have proved his innocence by carrying out what the Northern section of the army later demanded—the trial and punishment of Major Nzeogwu and his men.

Because of tribal prejudices these people have ignored the fact that the January coup, for all its faults, was nevertheless received with considerable enthusiasm in many quarters in Nigeria—especially among the youth who saw in it the beginning of a new era.

For Ironsi, at the time, to have gone beyond putting these boys in detention as he did, would almost certainly have provoked an anti-government reaction in many circles, especially in Southern Nigeria. Having himself narrowly escaped death at their hands, General Ironsi was hardly in love with these boys. But he had his dilemma. He was intensely conscious of the probable political consequences of any harsh attitude he might adopt towards them.

A similar situation recurred in July 1966 when the second coup took place. General Gowon, then lieutenant colonel, was General Ironsi's chief of staff when the "rebels" kidnapped the general along with Lt. Col. Adekunle Fajuyi from the latter's home. Brigadier Ogundipe, as General Ironsi's next-in-command, had assumed provisional leadership of the army. He believed Lt. Col. Gowon was on his side (General Gowon himself insists that he was and denies being party to the July plot), and sent him as a member of the Federal party appointed to negotiate with the "rebels," then under the leadership of Lt. Col. Murtala Mohamed. Lt. Col. Gowon came back riding high on the back of the "rebels" to assume command of the army and the leadership of the Federal Government. If, as General Gowon claims, probably with justification, we allow that he was not a party to the July plot, he can then be regarded as having been put in a position similar to that of General Ironsi in January 1966—suddenly heading a movement that was planned and launched by others. The questions that arise are therefore as follows:

1. If General Gowon is absolved from the crime of plotting the murder of his supreme commander, and if we accept his view that the leadership of the army and government was thrust upon him only after the act of rebellion which overthrew General Ironsi, why did he not punish the murderers of his supreme commander and the West Military Governor Lt. Col. Adekunle Fajuyi?

2. Why did he right from the start even go as far as meticulously avoiding the use of the word "rebels" for the perpetrators of the July coup?

3. Did he find it politically impossible to act against them?

4. Was he therefore in the same dilemma as General Ironsi found himself on assumption of office?

I will prefer to leave every Nigerian reader to try to think out the answers for himself or herself.

The objective being aimed at in this chapter, which I consider the most important in this book, is to show to fellow Nigerians and Nigeria's friends that the principal cause of our current tragedy is *bitterness born of misunderstanding*.

A misunderstanding of the motives behind the January coup led to the Northern revenge—or rather, "over-revenge"—as witnessed by the May riots, the July counter-coup and the massacres of September-October 1966. A similar misunderstanding of the intentions behind the actions of the Federal Government after these massacres led many Easterners, especially Ibos, to believe that what had happened was a planned attempt to exterminate them. I have gone to this length in trying to interpret the motives and probable intentions of the leaders of the January coup because of my conviction that our present tragedy stems directly from the confusion and misunderstanding which arose from that event.

If there is to be lasting settlement, our people of all tribes have to get right the ideas and ideals that moved these young men to act. It is rather their motives and intentions that we should judge, not the unfortunate outcome of a mismanaged attempt to achieve these motives. I believe that psychologically, in our new national setting, this is a vital point, the acceptance of which is a prerequisite to any meaningful advance towards national reconciliation and lasting peace.

> Our purpose was to change our country and make it a place we could be proud to call our home . . . Tribal considerations

were completely out of our minds. But we had a set-back in the execution.[2]

Major Chukwuma Kaduna Nzeogwu.

NOTES

1. Walter Schwarz, *Nigeria* (London and New York, 1968), pp. 193-198.
2. *Africa and the World*, vol. 3, no. 31, May 1967, p. 15.

CHAPTER 3

THE ARMY'S FAILINGS AND
POLITICAL FAILURES

In September 1966 I had occasion to discuss the confused situation in Nigeria with Brigadier Ogundipe, who after General
Ironsi's "disappearance," was then the most senior surviving officer
in the Nigerian army. He had come on a short visit to Paris just
before taking up his appointment as Nigeria's High Commissioner
in London. I expressed my regret at the fact that blood was shed
in January and again in May and July 1966. I asked if he did not
think that the cause of that tragedy was the failure on the part
of top indigenous army officers to act when they should. I cited
the example of the change of government in Pakistan in 1958,
when the then head of the army, Field Marshal Ayub Khan, led
his officers and men in a bloodless takeover of government. Also
mentioned was the removal from power of King Farouk in Egypt
in 1952 when General Neguib agreed with the young officers
under the inspiration of Col. Nasser to take over the government
of the country.

The point I was trying to make was that the army in Nigeria
appeared clearly too dense at the top to swing with the tempo of
the times, and that the failure of that top to lead the younger and
more volatile officers was largely responsible for the latter's
decision to take matters into their own hands. For these young
officers the task of overthrowing the government therefore,

necessarily involved the neutralization not only of the leaders of the government but also of the top layer of the army, whose weight and authority could have been used to checkmate their own efforts. Indeed, it was the survival of General Ironsi in January that was responsible for the collapse of the coup first of all in Lagos and ultimately in the whole country. Had he been liquidated along with the other senior army officers who suffered that unfortunate and most regrettable fate, probably the remainder of the troops would have been deprived of the strong rallying point which his position and prestige within the army provided.

Brigadier Ogundipe, who had listened quite patiently, thought for a while, shook his head and said, "The point you have just made appears very logical. Probably, you are right. I am aware of the examples of bloodless takeovers you have mentioned. Anyway, I must explain to you that it is not in the nature of officers with my upbringing to want to interfere in politics. We are taught to be good soldiers not politicians."

He may have been right professionally speaking, but tragic consequences arose from the failure of our top army leaders to appreciate the fact that when political recklessness becomes evident in the handling of the affairs of a young nation still in the process of formation, and where men charged with public affairs have no fixed rules of conduct, it may sometimes become the painful but salutary duty of the leadership of the army—the custodians of the nation's security—to call those engaged in the game to timely and effective attention.

With the January episode as the starting block in our *tragedy of errors*, vital weaknesses and indecision which marked General Ironsi's administration hastened the advent of further trouble. Unable to interpret the nation's political mood in the pre-coup era, General Ironsi quickly proved equally unable to manage the political situation produced by the coup. He was a non-political soldier who suddenly came to political office with an empty mind. In spite of this personal inadequacy, however, his regime might possibly have survived had it not found itself in an intolerable dilemma. Behind the facade of enthusiasm and general jubilation which greeted the January coup, there was the reality of an embittered North—the most powerful region in the Federation whose overall representation in the army itself kept good pace with its political dominance in the country. Northern interests had suffered heavily both on the political and the military planes. Once it recovered from the shock, the North was bound to seek to reassert itself in both domains. This it did in July 1966.

Even if General Ironsi had "tried and punished" the January boys as the North demanded there would still have been trouble. Not only would such an act have produced an immediate anti-government reaction from the South, sooner or later Northern political interests would have attempted to recover lost ground. The circumstances of the January coup and the one-sided killings that marked the coup's bloody aspect practically made such a situation inevitable.

Ironsi's acknowledged inability only made it quicker and easier.

The Counter-Coup of July 1966

The Federal Military Government has been considerably and consistently reticent about details of what happened during the counter-coup of July 1966. In its important publication—*Nigeria 1966*—which appeared in January 1967 (that is six months after the coup), and which gave a review of the events of 1966, it had only the following to record:

> There were wildly circulating rumours that the "uncompleted" job of January 15 was to be finished by eliminating the remaining officers of non-Eastern origin. Although many top Army officers of non-Eastern origin had been killed in January, there were others who luckily escaped being murdered. Some of these were out of Nigeria in January 1966, and have since returned to the

country. They were now holding some key positions in the Army and still prevented a complete all-Ibo affair at the top of the Military Administration.

There were also rumours of a counter-coup planned by some Northern elements in the Army with the assistance of civilians.

On July 28 there was strong evidence that one group or the other would attempt something but the details were not available to the senior officers. The Supreme Headquarters and the Army Headquarters took the normal military precaution of warning all units to remain alert. It appears, from the investigations, that an officer in Abeokuta went beyond the precautionary measure and armed some men drawn from Southern rank and file. When those of Northern origin got wind of this they became apprehensive of such a move, thinking a repeat of 15th January, 1966, was in the offing. They also took their weapons. These latter men shot three of their officers on the spot and in-fighting within the Army spread to Ibadan, Ikeja and then the units stationed in the North followed.

The disorder in the Army continued all over the week-end after the former Supreme Commander Major-General Aguiyi-Ironsi and the Military Governor, West, had been kidnapped at the Government House, Ibadan.[1]

In another publication, *Background Notes on the Nigerian Crisis,* issued in October 1967, it had just the following to say:

> Several causes led to the revolt of July 29, 1966, against General Ironsi's regime. Firstly, for more than six months, junior officers who had killed more than a dozen senior Northern military officers were not court-martialled and disciplined in any way. Secondly, there were persistent rumours of an Ibo Master Plan "to complete the job" of January 15 by killing the surviving Northern officers. Thirdly, the promotion of 23 Army officers of whom 19 were Ibos appeared to be part of the plan. To cap it all, General Ironsi promulgated the Decree abolishing the Federal System of Government. The revolt of July appeared to be aimed only at removing the threat from the Ibo officer class. *It is important to stress that no civilian was killed in the revolt.* It is clear therefore that the revolt of July 29 was not a Northern Master Plan to kill all Ibos and dominate the country.[2]

The Eastern Nigerian Government account is understandably much fuller. Below is an extract from the publication—*January 15. Before and After*—issued early in 1967.

The 2nd Brigade in the South

Abeokuta

As had been pre-arranged by the conspirators, the signal for the massacre of Army officers and men of Eastern and Mid-Western origin was given at Abeokuta in Western Nigeria. At about 11 P.M. on July 28, 1966, two sections of Northern troops at Abeokuta broke into a meeting of officers in the officers' Mess and shot Major Obienu, Lt. Orok and Lt. Col. Okonweze—all officers of Eastern and Mid-Western origin; and then besieged the rest of the barracks. While the siege was in progress the Northern troops disarmed the Southern soldiers among the guards, broke into the armoury and magazine, distributed arms and ammunition to more Northern troops, and sounded an alarm for action. Many soldiers in answer to the alarm assembled, but Southern soldiers among them were arrested and detained in the Guardroom and in the armoury which was now converted into a guardroom. Troops of Northern origin then went from door to door in the barracks in search of troops of Southern origin who did not answer the alarm. Some of those caught were manhandled and pushed into the Guardrooms while others were shot at sight. Others still were got at in some civilians' houses near the barracks. A vehicle was parked near one of the unoccupied married officers' quarters, and into this vehicle were dumped the bodies of the Southern officers and men as they were killed. By daybreak most of the Southern senior Non-Commissioned Officers were brought out of the guardroom and shot in the open and their bodies dumped in the storage vehicle.

Ibadan

At Ibadan news of the "mutiny" at Abeokuta was conveyed, soon after it was received in the early hours of July 29, to General Ironsi, who was staying at Government House with his host, Lt. Col. Adekunle Fajuyi, the Military Governor of Western Nigeria. In the Supreme Commander's entourage was also Lt. Col. H. M. Njoka, Officer Commanding the 2nd Brigade. The three senior officers quickly conferred and decided that Lt. Col. Njoku should proceed to Lagos in plain clothes and in a civilian vehicle to take over control and counter the "mutiny."

But soon after leaving Government House for his chalet Lt.

Col. Njoku noticed troops dismounting from two Land Rovers and the silhouette of the Aide-de-Camp to the Military Governor of the West, who directed the soldiers' attention to the Lt. Col. Immediately two or three soldiers in the gang fired at him from Sten guns and he returned the fire with his pistol. Shot in the thigh and elsewhere, Lt. Col. Njoku escaped in helpless condition and made for the University College Hospital, Ibadan, where he was admitted for treatment. There again he was attacked by the assassins, but he escaped and eventually found his way to the East.

Before midnight on July 28-29, the Southern troops in the Supreme Commander's bodyguard had been removed and disarmed, and soon the Northerners among the body-guard were reinforced by a special contingent of twenty-four Northern soldiers from the 4th Battalion at Ibadan under the over-all command of Major T. Y. Danjuma. Before midnight, too, the whole of Government House had been besieged and the Supreme Commander, his host and others of his party were virtually under house arrest; while Lt. Bello, the Military Aide-de-Camp to the Supreme Commander, and the Aide-de-Camp to the Military Governor of the West were difficult to get at.

Consequently Lt. Nwankwo, the Supreme Commander's Air-force A. D. C., was sent downstairs to check on the state of affairs outside the House, but he was arrested and detained by the mutinous guards. Then, after waiting for a long time, Lt. Col. Fajuyi walked down to find out what had happened to Lt. Nwankwo, and he himself was also arrested and detained. Finally, at about 9 A.M. (July 29), Major Danjuma took some of his men upstairs, confronted and questioned the Supreme Commander, saluted him, and ordered his arrest. The Supreme Commander was led downstairs to join the other two captives. The three captives were now stripped and their hands tied behind their backs with wire. They were flogged, tortured and then put into separate Police vans.

The whole convoy now moved, with Major Danjuma leading. On arrival at the Mokola junction of the Letmauk barracks and Oyo roads, Major Danjuma signalled to the rest of the convoy to proceed while he himself made for the barracks.

After travelling for about ten miles on the Ibadan-Iwo road the convoy stopped at a prearranged spot. The captives were ordered out and led along a footpath off the right side of the road. The special team for these final operations were now Lt. Walbe, Lt. Paiko, Warrant Officer (W.O.) I. Bako, Company Sergeant-Major (C.S.M.) Useni Fegge, and a few others. These

Northern Officers and men beat and tortured the captives so badly that their bodies were swollen and bleeding profusely. The Supreme Commander and the Western Military Governor, both of whom could hardly walk any more, fell over several times but were taken up and ordered to continue walking. When they got to a stream flowing across the path and could not leap over, they were pushed across and fell over. They were taken up again, carried a few paces beyond the stream, laid face downwards and given a final beating. At this stage the Airforce Aide-de-Camp to the Supreme Commander managed to escape. The Supreme Commander and the Western Military Governor, who were almost dead by now, were separately finished by a few rounds of machine-gun fire. In the evening of the same day some Northern soldiers returned to the spot and covered the two dead bodies with earth scraped from the ground around them. Some five days later the Special Branch of the Nigeria Police dug up the bodies, identified them, and buried them in the Military Cemetery, Ibadan. After the burial an identification mark was planted on each grave. It was these marks that eventually helped to identify the bodies when they were exhumed in January, 1967 for re-burial in the respective home-towns of the Supreme Commander and the Western Nigeria Military Governor.

Ikeja

Of the ghastly events that took place in military stations in various parts of Nigeria on July 29 and after, those that occurred at Ikeja are the most remarkable because there the annihilation of Eastern officers and men was most complete and the atrocities most horrible to relate.

Before midnight on July 28-29, Lt. Col. Mohammed, Major Alao and Major Martin Adamu alerted and addressed the Northern soldiers in secret and spurred them on to action. Then followed the usual disarming of Southern troops, the seizure of the armoury and magazines and the distribution of arms and ammunition among Northern soldiers. To this was added the disruption of the communication system.

Subsequently, in the early hours of July 29, troops from Abeokuta (presumably those who had come to reconnoitre a few days earlier), under 2nd Lt. Longboem, surrounded the house of the Commanding Officer, Lt. Col. Henry Igboba, who, however, fled to safety. Other officers of Eastern origin were trapped in their houses or captured elsewhere in the barracks and killed. As for other ranks of Eastern origin, at about 5 A.M. the Northern soldiers surrounded the Quartermasters' department and all approaches to the training area from the quarters of other ranks. The Northern soldiers were armed with rifles and machine-guns which made it difficult for anyone to escape. At about 6:30 A.M. the signal shot was fired in the area of the Commanding Officer's house, and there immediately followed continuous firing in various directions, particularly in the quarters of other ranks. Troops going out on physical training were intercepted and the Easterners among them were shot or locked up in the Guardroom. Later the captives were led out in groups and shot in the open in the full view of those still in detention.

The operations of the Northern troops at Ikeja were extended to the general public in a manner not practised elsewhere on July 29. Members of the Nigeria Police Force, customs officials and other civilians on the highway leading to the Airport were arrested and taken to the barracks for detention. Before mid-day over 200 persons, soldiers and civilians, had been detained in the Guardroom.

But the most horrible and repulsive aspect of this shocking story was the atrocities committed against the captives before they were killed. There was one special case which stood out from the rest. Capt. P. C. Okoye, who was on his way to attend a course in the United States, was caught at Ikeja Airport, tied to an iron cross, beaten most severely with horse-whip (koboko), and (still on the cross), thrown into the Guardroom where his body got so badly swollen that he died.[2]

The 1st Brigade in the North

Generally, operations in the North did not start until about twenty-four hours after they had begun in the South. Troops of the Reconnaissance Squadron, the Field Battery and the 3rd Battalion—all in Kaduna—were extensively used in the initial operations, though Northern troops in various other units also carried out independent assignments and raids later.

Kaduna

At the 1st Brigade Headquarters, Kaduna, on the night of July 29, Captain Eket and six other Eastern officers were arrested and taken to Kakuri. On July 30 all other officers of Southern origin were arrested, flogged, tortured and placed under guard. On

August 1 the Eastern officers were taken from Kakuri back to Headquarters, questioned, sentenced to death by Major Kyari, and again placed under guard. On August 2 the Western officers among those arrested on July 30 were released.

On the same day, August 2, the Eastern officers under sentence of death were driven out, under the charge of Captain Ahmadu Yakubu, along the Kaduna-Jos Road. There, at a spot some nineteen miles from Kaduna, was stationed a firing squad. At about 12:10 P.M. all the Eastern officers were shot.

In the Barracks at Headquarters, until August 5, most soldiers of Eastern origin were harassed, tortured and in some cases killed. Others were arrested and taken to Kaduna prisons. One significant feature of the Northern operations was this remarkable cooperation between the military and civil authorities.

In the 3rd Battalion Barracks at Kawo, Kaduna, the Commanding Officer, Lt. Col. I. C. Okoro spoke to the troops at about 1 P.M. on July 29. He exhorted them to be loyal and not to be disturbed by the reported mutiny in the South. Later in the evening the Regimental Sergeant-Major, Ahmadu Bello, telephoned the Commanding Officer about the internal security situation and asked if he could come to the area of the Guardroom. On his arrival there in answer to the call Lt. Col. Okoro was questioned and shot by two of his young officers Lt. Dambo and Lt. Dinka. Captain Swanton, a Northerner, now took over command of the 3rd Battalion and co-ordinated his activities with those of the 1st Brigade Headquarters.

At about 6:30 A.M. on July 30 an alarm was sounded and all troops assembled at the hockey pitch only to realize that the place had been surrounded by Northern troops. Soon after Southern soldiers were mown down by rifle and machine-gun fire. Then the soldiers' quarters were surrounded and the telephone exchange room taken. It was the timely intervention of Captain Swanton and the Regimental Sergeant-Major that saved some Southerners from extermination at the hockey pitch. Subsequently those who had escaped death were severely beaten and detained in the cinema hall which was surrounded by armed Northern soldiers. Later the Westerners among the detainees were separated from the Easterners. More people were afterwards brought into the hall from other units in Kaduna, so that by the second day there were about 250 Easterners in the hall.[3]

The two accounts given above about the events of July 1966 reflect the contradictory views of the two sides in the present conflict. The Eastern Regional Government, whose people were the principal victims, took great pains to give details of those events as seen by Easterners. I have no intention here to argue anybody's case but there is little doubt that the killings of July 1966 were grossly out of proportion with what happened during the January episode.

In its own account (published in *Nigeria 1966*), the Federal Military Government recorded only a total of 15 people killed throughout the country.

> The mutinous activities of January 15 resulted in the death of seven people in Lagos, including the Prime Minister, Alhaji Sir Abubakar Tafawa Balewa, his Minister of Finance, Chief F. S. Okotie-Eboh, and five senior Military Officers, the Premier of Western Region, Chief S. L. Akintola (killed in Ibadan); seven people in Kaduna including the Premier, Alhaji Sir Ahmadu Bello, Brigadier S. A. Ademulegun and his wife.[4]

This figure hardly compares with the total of 214 persons killed in July. Walter Schwarz in characteristic laconic style puts the equation as follows: "If the July Coup was intended primarily for revenge, it was singularly successful."[5]

In spite of the exaggerated tone of the "Northern revenge" things did not get out of control in July. It was principally the subsequent political mistakes of the new administration that turned the vast majority of Ibos against the Federal Military Government. These mistakes were in turn to shift the ground for suspicion from the Northern camp to the Eastern camp. What had happened notwithstanding, many Southerners and indeed many Ibos, while they were gravely distressed by the slaughter of Southern but mainly Ibo officers, were still disposed to regard the event as a largely military affair, a sort of return match by which Northern military officers provoked by the January coup sought to score even with their Southern and especially Eastern counterparts.

But after killing General Ironsi and Lt. Col. Fajuyi, the rebellious officers were determined to have things their own way to the extent that in their view no Southern officer was worthy enough to be entrusted with the government of the nation. Brigadier Ogundipe and other senior Southern army officers who came next in rank to General Ironsi were left in no doubt as to their unsuitability for the leadership of either the army or the country. Only a Northerner was acceptable. It was thus that the mantle of government fell on the shoulders of the most senior Northern officer in the Nigerian army, then Lt. Col. Yakubu Gowon, who at that time had at least six surviving Southern officers including Lt. Col. Odumegwu Ojukwu above him in military seniority.

Even at this stage many Southerners, including many moderate Ibos, grieved as they were by the revengeful undertone of the July coup, were still ready to make allowance in their minds that the Northern attitude was a reaction—many believed it was an overreaction—to the allegedly "Ibo" coup of January. They were still prepared to cooperate with the Federal Government to bring about peace and settlement in the country.

It was not until the renewed outbreak of violence in September-October 1966 in most parts of Northern Nigeria, against civilian masses—men, women and even children—of Southern but especially Ibo origin, that moderate Ibos began to feel that what was happening was not just a spilling over of Northern anger provoked by the January coup, but was a deliberate attempt to eliminate the Ibos as a people. The Federal Government at this very juncture failed to convince them that this was not the case. It failed for example to make meaningful financial provision for the families and dependants of those who lost their lives or to help resettle the multitude of refugees impoverished by their losses. It promised to make available the sum of 300,000 pounds—a paltry amount when compared with one million pounds voted outright by Lt. Col. Ojukwu's East Regional Government.

While individual Nigerians and various organizations including the venerable Obas and Chiefs of Western Nigeria abundantly demonstrated their concern and their grief, the Federal Government demonstrated what in many Ibo minds was an astonishingly callous indifference to the fate of their kinsmen. This default on the part of the Federal Government stirred in the minds of many moderate Ibos the feeling that the administration in Lagos could not possibly be for them, but that it was in fact against them. At this point it was immaterial to the Ibos what the intentions of General Gowon and his advisers may have been, just as it had proved immaterial to the Northerners what the intentions of Major Nzeogwu and his group of January 1966 might have been. The important thing is that the impression was clearly created and embedded in the Ibo mind that Ibos as a people were no longer wanted or cared for. Many of them had expected the Federal Government to act swiftly and conduct itself in such a way as to show that it was the caretaker of the nation as a whole and to demonstrate that what was happening was, in its view, a quarrel between two sections of the country and not between the Federal Government itself and a section of the country. General Gowon's government did very little to create this much desired impression, at least in the minds of millions of Ibos. Instead, by its gross omissions in this respect, it left the impression that the Federal Government was not much more than an extension of the Northern Government.

At a time when the relatively much poorer East Regional Government was able to provide an initial amount of one million pounds for the rehabilitation of refugees, who had come seeking safety and shelter denied them elsewhere in what was supposed to be their own country, the Federal Government promised only 300,000 pounds. This amount, when spread over the estimated two million refugees at the time, would come to a little over 2s. 6d. (25¢) per refugee. How far could half-a-crown have gone in helping to tackle effectively the problem of an individual faced with the task of resettling himself? It was about this same time that news spread of an arms deal between the Federal Government and foreign firms involving the alleged amount of eight million pounds!* True or false many people believed this story. In the minds of such people the apparent disparity between what the Federal Government was ready to spend on resettling displaced Easterners on the one hand, and on arms on the other, was very disturbing. It became impossible to reassure many Ibos of the honest intentions of the federal authorities towards them and their tragedy-stricken kinsmen.

It was felt in most Ibo circles that a government which held the national umbrella had the moral duty to prove that it was holding the same over the heads of everybody in need, and that no one in its care was left to die drenched in the rain. It was this vital default after the September-October massacres by which the Federal Government failed in the eyes of even the most moderate Ibos to rise to the national level, but still appeared chained to the parochial prejudices of a particular region, that broke the unity of the country. Many Ibos began to feel that they had no choice but to support their people in the struggle for survival. This determination and the psychological state it produced, led to the feverish preparation for their own security. I still feel that those who run the affairs of the Federal Government have not fully absorbed this important lesson. Otherwise, how can the government continue to say it is merely crushing a military rebellion when in fact it is emasculating and strangling a whole people? The total blockade by sea, air and land which has been on for the past twenty months remains morally condemnable and politically inexcusable.† We are today all living witnesses of the

---

* This matter was subsequently raised by Lt. Col. Ojukwu at the Aburi Conference and General Gowon disclaimed knowledge of any deal of that magnitude.

† The Red Cross and other charity organisations have since been able to fly in supplies but so far no agreement has been reached with regard to land and sea transportation.

effect of the blockade on hundreds of thousands of innocent little children. One can understand and appreciate the necessity for a partial blockade imposed strictly on the importation of arms into the country, but which makes practical allowance for food and medicine to come to innocent people in need. Such a step would surely have been more in keeping with General Gowon's promise of *police action*. The total blockade such as we see, involving the importation of drugs and food, has clearly no place in a conflict that is supposed to be between brothers of one and the same country. It has not helped to convince the ordinary man in Biafra that the issue is just an affair designed to crush the military rebellion of "Ojukwu and his clique." If, as I believe many Nigerians are, we are all anxious and sincere in desiring peace, then the time has come for us to begin to think seriously and differently.

True unity cannot be built upon the domination of one section of the country by another, as was so clearly proved by the collapse of the old federation. It cannot either be built on the military conquest of one section by another, as is now being unwisely attempted.

For durable peace and stability, the outcome of the present bitter and wasteful experience should produce neither victor nor vanquished. The memory left should be that of an unfortunate but basically unavoidable trial of strength—an explosion of forces built up over the years by rival but not intrinsically incompatible interests. The lesson to be learned, and this should be a permanent one, must be that the regulation of affairs and the settlement of differences between peoples who are forced by geography, and indeed, in the larger African context by consanguinity, to live together, cannot profitably depend on the employment of naked force. As in the case of children born of the same parents, a neighbour is one who often by chance and rarely by choice you find next to you and who is in consequence close to your everyday life. For peace and progress in our country, we all have a duty to begin seriously to learn (and it takes not only talent but moral courage to do this) to tolerate something of our neighbour's idiosyncrasies.

NOTES

1. *Nigeria 1966,* no. NNPG/114/66/10,000 (Federal Ministry of Information, Lagos, 1967), p. 9.
2. *Background Notes on the Nigerian Crisis,* no. DPDL/1067/10,000 (Federal Ministry of Information, Lagos, October 1967), p. 4.
3. *January 15. Before and After,* no. WT/1003/3674/40,000, 1967 (Eastern Regional Government publication). Also in *1966. Nigerian crisis,* vol. 7 (Enugu, 1966), p. 44.
4. Walter Schwarz, *Nigeria* (London and New York, 1968), p. 7.
5. Ibid., p. 211.

Chapter 4

SECESSION AND THE PROBLEM OF MINORITIES

> Great empires and little minds go
> ill together.
>
> Edmund Burke

The two extracts below, culled from the papers submitted by the Nigerian and Biafran delegations to the Addis Ababa Peace Conference (August 1968), represent the standard *prise de position* of the contending parties vis-à-vis the causes and import of secession.

Abortive Efforts by General Gowon to Appease Ojukwu

It is necessary at this stage to recall the long history of efforts at conciliation from October, 1966 to May, 1967. The decision of the Federal Military Government, even when there was no military capacity in the East, to refrain from action against the illegal actions and defiance of Federal Government's authority by Mr. Ojukwu, illustrates clearly the conciliatory approach of the Federal Government.

In spite of the following outrageous acts directed by Mr. Ojukwu, the Federal Government continued its efforts to persuade the East to see reason and co-operate:

The seizure within the Region of more than one-third of the rolling stock of the Nigerian Railway, including 800 wagons and 115 oil tankers;

The denial of port facilities to exports from the Northern Region;

Persistent obstruction of the movement to the North of oil products from the Refinery (owned by all the Governments in Nigeria, including that of the Northern Region);

The seizure of property belonging to a foreign government—the neighbouring Republic of Chad;

The seizure of barge-borne traffic on the international waterway of the River Niger bound for the friendly Republics of Niger and Cameroun;

The expulsion since October, 1966, of all non-Easterners from the East;

All these outrageous acts were overlooked by the Federal Government in the belief that time was needed for Mr. Ojukwu and his group to come round to discuss how best to restore the country to normal conditions.

Again, after the Aburi Conference held in Ghana in January 1967 a Decree (No. 8)* was introduced which completely decentralized the country even beyond the original demands of Mr. Ojukwu and beyond the provisions of the Nigerian Federal Constitution. The Decree was unacceptable to Ojukwu because it contained a clause which provided against secession.

One by one, these efforts were completely frustrated by Mr. Ojukwu and his group who, from the very beginning, had set their minds on secession. More regrettably, the long time spent in genuinely trying to appease them was used by them to engage in a massive arms build-up in preparation for Civil War.

Biafra Did Not Secede

It is necessary, therefore, to examine what is called secession or rebellion in the Nigeria-Biafra crisis. We exhibit as Appendix I a copy of our Declaration of Independence on 30th May 1967. It contains the reasons for the Declaration which may be summarized thus:

(I) The pogrom of 1966 which took place in Northern Nigeria, and the persecution and terrorising of Eastern Nigerians which ensued in other parts of Nigeria, drove all living Eastern Nigerians from Northern, Western and Mid-Western Nigeria back to Eastern Nigeria. The relevance of this fact is two-fold. Firstly, from then onward, Eastern Nigeria, not Nigeria as a whole, became for Eastern Nigerians the only safe abode, their home-land.

* See Appendix B.

Secondly, those Eastern Nigerians who could not run away from the slaughter and persecution went from one hideout to another until, for purely propaganda purposes, their persecution was relaxed. Those who were thus stranded outside their Eastern Nigeria home-land were made to register and carry passes in Lagos and other parts of Nigeria where they found themselves. No other group in Nigeria was made to register or carry passes in this way. This showed that Eastern Nigerians were certainly not regarded as citizens of Nigeria.

(II) Then came a series of economic acts calculated to aggravate the unfortunate plight of Eastern Nigerians. Notable examples are the food blockade in October 1966, and the subsequent economic blockade of Eastern Nigeria by air, land and sea. There was also Nigeria's refusal to pay to Eastern Nigeria her lawful share of statutory revenue totalling about £12 million. Added to these, statutory corporations in Eastern Nigeria were denied access to spare parts and other facilities for the servicing of their undertakings; and public servants in Federal employment who fled back to Eastern Nigeria were denied their emoluments.

(III) These were followed by the application of political sanctions which struck at the very root of common citizenship. One example was the withdrawal of Nigerian passports to persons of Eastern Nigeria origin, and attempts to induce several nations not to permit Eastern Nigerians to enter their territories. Another instance was the attempt to impose a twelve-state structure, dividing Eastern Nigeria into three states without consultation, contrary to Lt.-Col. Gowon's Decree No. 8.

(IV) Postal, telegraphic and transport services between the rest of Nigeria and Eastern Nigeria were stopped by Lt.-Col. Gowon. It may be recalled that Lt.-Col. Gowon had, by then, been collecting arms and training soldiers for an attack on Eastern Nigeria. In Decree No. 8, he took upon himself powers to declare a state of emergency in any part of the country. This, as events later proved, was directed against Eastern Nigeria. It may be recalled also that Chief Obafemi Awolowo declared publicly that he had discovered plans, concluded by Lagos, for pushing Eastern Nigeria out of the Federation.

This was the state of affairs on 30th May 1967. Eastern Nigeria had, by the acts of Lt.-Col. Gowon, been pushed out of Nigeria, and, yet, was not a state by herself. It was a situation which could hardly be tolerated, and the Declaration of 30th May 1967, authorized by all Biafrans, was merely intended to regularize the position. There was neither secession nor rebellion.

For the Federal Government of Nigeria the secession of the

Eastern Region—Biafra—was the natural and inevitable culmination of a carefully laid out plan nurtured secretly to maturity. For Biafra, she was rejected and "pushed out" of Nigeria.

The truth is somewhere in between these two distinct and conflicting positions. Biafra had a plan for secession but it had not matured by May 1967, and secession could have been averted had the Federal Government shown greater appreciation of the feelings in the East following the "adulteration" of the *Aburi accord*. Instead it lost its nerve, panicked, and in an attempt to forestall, it precipitated secession. But the ease and rapidity with which the East was "pushed over" and out of the Federation also demonstrates how close she had brought herself to the edge of secession.

There can be little doubt that the important decision to secede was not arrived at overnight. It was preceded by some preparation. Dr. Graham-Douglas, formerly Attorney General in the East makes this assertion in his pamphlet *Ojukwu's Rebellion and World Opinion*.[2] As early as March 1967 an official of the Eastern Regional Government, intercepted at London airport, was found with designs and specimens of currency notes and stamps for the Republic of Biafra. The British customs officials there borrowed the documents for some five hours for "routine scrutiny" before returning them to the frightened traveller.

Lagos was not kept in the dark about this incident. But to say that secession was being prepared is not to say that it was at that time unavoidable.

The truth is that in the East there were two definite tendencies which cut through both the civilian population and the army itself. While the Eastern population at large—Ibos and the minorities alike—was seething with anger and thirsting for revenge after the massacre of 1966, the intelligentsia were busy thinking how to tackle the problem of ensuring the security of the region against further threats from the North.

Certain "diehards," found especially among top civil servants who had fled Lagos, pressed for complete separation from Nigeria. Many other Easterners—mainly from the business community—advised caution. This second group, disappointed as it was with what practically every informed Easterner regarded as the failure of the Federal Government to implement the *Aburi accord*, was nevertheless hoping for some last minute compromise settlement.

Because the "discredited" politicians were methodically left out of the show (a number of them including the erstwhile Premier of the Eastern Region, Dr. Michael Okpara, were imprisoned), the government of the region was robbed of the politicians' most important asset—supple realism. The void thus created greatly enhanced the voice and the chances of the "diehards" who, despite their proven ability in the relatively closed world of the civil service and academics, were novices in the tortuous game of politics.

The army itself was divided. Even after the Aburi fiasco a number of high-ranking officers, determined as they undoubtedly were to fight back and redeem their honour sullied by their Northern counterparts in July 1966, were nevertheless wary about the military and political hazards implicit in an outright and ill-prepared secession.

This group included the most senior surviving Ibo officer (senior to Lt. Col. Ojukwu), Brigadier Hilary Njoku. He was with General Ironsi at Ibadan on the fateful night of 28th July 1966, when the latter was kidnapped and killed by rebellious Northern troops. He narrowly escaped death after having collected eight shrapnels in one of his thighs. It was he who reorganized the straggling Eastern soldiers that came home after the July coup, and as commanding officer, launched what became the Biafran army. After a few serious internal clashes with Lt. Col. Ojukwu over control of the army, he was arrested and put in "protective custody" in October 1967. He was not accused of sabotage. (Brigadier Njoku was released by General Effiong in January 1970, two days after General Ojukwu fled Biafra.)

53

Reportedly sharing Brigadier Njoku's views was Major Chuk-wuma Kaduna Nzeogwu, the leader of the January coup who, following the July counter-coup, was released from detention where Ironsi had put him. Very little was known of his views until his release. Below is a record of what he had to say regarding secession as reported during an interview which he accorded to Dennis Ejindu in *Africa and the World*.

> *Ejindu:* From the present chaos, what type of Nigeria do you envisage?
> *Nzeogwu:* In the first place, secession will be ill-advised, indeed impossible. Even if the East fights a' war of secession and wins, it still cannot secede. Personally, I don't like secession and if the country disintegrates, I shall pack up my things and go. In the present circumstances, confederation is the best answer as a temporary measure. In time, we shall have complete unity. Give this country a confederation and, believe me, in ten or fifteen years the young men will find it intolerable, and will get together to change it. And it is obvious we shall get a confederation or something near it. Nothing will stop that.[3]

Nzeogwu's Release from Prison

The following question and answer regarding the circumstances of his release are also interesting.

> *Ejindu:* Finally, let me come to the controversy over your release. Much as it has been a popular action you have been re-leased by the East Government against the wish of the Federal Government. What do you say to that?
> *Nzeogwu:* All I can say is that I am happy and grateful to be out. We feel grateful to the Nsukka students for their persistent demand, and to the boys in the barracks for their pressure on the authorities in the East. And to the Nigerian public in general for their concern over our welfare.[4]

The above would appear to add credence to widely held views that the East Regional Governor, Lt. Col. Ojukwu, did never really reconcile himself to the idea of accommodating Major

Nzeogwu—a unique personality of whom the following has been said:

> Major Nzeogwu at 29, is reputed to be one of the few astute soldiers Nigeria has ever produced, and probably will ever do. Adored in the ranks for his bravery and informality and respected (even feared) by his officer-colleagues for his skill and persuasive ability, he is the one soldier in Nigeria whose name at once invokes hatred and awe.[5]

After the interview quoted above, he fell out of grace with Lt. Col. Ojukwu. When other officers of his rank and even those with whom he had been in detention were promoted, he was skipped. He was actually on "leave" when the war broke out. He died in mysterious circumstances very early in the war on the Nsukka front shortly before Biafra's thrust into his home region, the Mid-West—a campaign which many people knew was being prepared, and most expected him naturally to lead. His body was found by Northern soldiers who took it away and announced that it would be buried with military honours in Kaduna, at the same time as the Biafran government denied that he was dead.

Brigadier George Kurubo, formerly Chief of the Air Force in General Ironsi's government, although a non-Ibo, was one of the strongest opponents of the July counter-coup. He was among the earliest to run back to the Eastern Region to give his support to Lt. Col. Ojukwu. He was later to take the opportunity of a mission abroad in June 1967, to quit the Biafran side. (He is currently Nigeria's ambassador in Moscow.) He told me in Paris, weeks before he switched over, that he was for a fight against that section of the army which killed General Ironsi but that he was against secession from Nigeria and had told Lt. Col. Ojukwu so. Indeed it was widely known that most of the "January boys" then in the Biafran army were much more interested in "completing their job" and giving a fight to the Northern soldiers than in the purely political approach as represented by secession.

The following was part of a protracted and systematic attempt to suppress resistance or suspicion of resistance to the "people's" choice to secede:

1. The public execution of three senior army officers (22nd of September 1967) after the Mid-West debacle (Biafran forces were beaten back)
   a. Lt. Col. Banjo (a Yoruba from the West)
   b. Lt. Col. Emmanuel Ifeajuna (one of the "January boys" and an Ibo from the East)
   c. Major Alele (a non-Ibo Mid-Westerner who had given his support to Lt. Col. Ojukwu after the July coup)
   d. Mr. Sam Ironka Agbam (a young Ibo foreign service officer who was one of the first diplomats to quit Lagos and declare for Lt. Col. Ojukwu)
2. The reported private execution of a number of other military officers including Major Ademuyega (the brilliant young graduate of Ibadan and Major Nzeogwu's close friend)
3. The "sabotage" witch-hunt that followed practically every Biafran military reverse even up to the fall of Port Harcourt in May 1968
4. The numerous arrests and summary detentions of young intellectuals including a number of lawyers from Onitsha.

After the September-October massacres the role of the masses in the Eastern Region had become that of a potent catalyst. While they took no direct part in decisions, their ugly mood, their fears and their intense determination to fight were a ready instrument for any one willing to risk an arduous gamble. They were ready for any tough line, any defiance directed against the North or what they saw as the North's agent—the Federal *équipe* in Lagos.

Lt. Col. Ojukwu's personal position at the beginning is not quite clear. But there are signs that he hesitated considerably before taking the plunge for secession. Pressured by articulate and in some cases interested diehard "returnees" and "escapees" to secede, with the politicians in cold storage now assured of powerful and uncritical mass support for any "tough" decision, and finally himself vastly under-estimating the military and international implications of secession, Lt. Col. Ojukwu appeared to have leaned increasingly towards the hard liners and needed only a modicum of provocation to act. This provocation was readily supplied by the Federal Government's decree of 27th May splitting the whole country into twelve states.

Intended as an act to forestall the East's secession (that was clearly brewing) by detaching Eastern minority support from Lt. Col. Ojukwu's government, that decree precipitated secession. It angered even the moderates among the Ibo civilians, who lost their voice at once. As Lt. Col. Ojukwu kept political decisions to himself, it is not clear how much the army's opinion was formally or seriously sought.

With the parallel existence of pro-secessionist and anti-secessionist tendencies even when dissatisfaction was at its height, it is most probable that by May 1967 the "secession process" had not really taken an irreversible course. It appears that like his brilliant manipulation of military threats, such as stating that he was in a position to "line the bottom of the sea with the debris of the Nigerian navy," and that "no power in black Africa" could face the Biafran military strength, Lt. Col. Ojukwu was magnifying the threat of secession as a means to squeeze concessions out of Lagos.

The frequent mass rallies organized by government agents and masterminded by Mr. Alele, a superb socialist agitator who learned his trade in Moscow (he was later at the outbreak of war given a temporary commission as a Major in the army and was to die afterwards in circumstances I have already mentioned); the "unanimous" Assembly resolutions urging a break with Nigeria—

all these were part of the future Biafran leader's attempt to impress the Federal Government with the seriousness of the situation.

On this, as on the military plane, Lagos took him at his word and reacted accordingly. By May 1967 there were clearly two strings to the Eastern Nigerians bow. But the fact that the first shot was taken with the one marked with secession was decided by circumstances.

If the Federal Government had not lost its nerve, secession might have been averted. The only thing that was clearly inevitable was fighting—an armed clash between sections of a broken army. For the bulk of the Eastern soldiers and their leaders, like Brigadiers Njoku and Kurubo, there was need to redeem their honour. For the "January boys" like Major Nzeogwu, Lt. Col. Ifeajuna or Lt. Col. Banjo, the "job" had to be completed. That this fight became a fight for secession was Lt. Col. Ojukwu's political decision. Even when the fight had begun, as events were later to prove, neither of these groups felt fully within themselves that they were fighting for secession.

As we have tried to illustrate above, the declaration of secession by the Eastern Region of Nigeria on 30th May 1967 was a direct reaction to the Federal Government's promulgation of the twelve-state decree which divided not only the rest of Nigeria into nine states but the Eastern Region into three states. This division was carried out without consulting and therefore without the consent of the Military Government of the Eastern Region. The abrupt and unilateral manner in which it was done was an open challenge to both the government and people of Eastern Nigeria as it was in direct opposition to the rules of procedure expected of a far-seeing government at the centre. Military government is not synonymous with selective dictatorship. It may, and often it does, imply a strong or harsh government. But such strong or harsh measures are expected to be uniformly applied to all concerned. Within the army itself a military government has certain obligations to respect. General Ironsi, as Supreme Commander, did promulgate decrees affecting the whole country, but all these decrees, including the ill-fated Decree No. 34, which set aside the regional structure, were passed after consultations and without evident opposition from any Military Governor.

It is therefore clear that in view of the above precedent, especially after the Aburi Conference which had provided that—

> The legislative and executive authority of the Federal Military Government should be vested in the Supreme Military Council to which any decision affecting the whole country should be referred for determination, providing that where it is not possible for a meeting to be held the matter requiring determination should be referred to the Military Governors for their comments and concurrence.[6]

—any awkwardly handled decision by the Federal Government on such a far-reaching issue was bound to provoke trouble.

Federal defenders of this action readily point to Lt. Col. Ojukwu's "intransigence" and refusal to cooperate with the Federal authorities over the vexed issue of interpretation and implementation of the *Aburi accord*. They claim thus that the Federal Government was left with no choice but to act without the consent of the East Military Government.

The East Military Government for its part, in answer to the charge of obstructing the Federal Government, has blamed the situation on what it considered the betrayal of the *Aburi spirit* by the Federal Government. Numerous publications have since been issued by each side to prove how justified its conduct had been.

Decree No. 8 and Federal Efforts at Conciliation

Promulgated on 10th March 1967 at Benin, Decree No. 8 was an attempt by the Federal Military Government to implement the *Aburi* decisions. It deserves special examination since it was a veritable climax in the confusion that followed the diverse interpretations of *Aburi*. Once it failed to score, it became clear to all observers that a clash between the Federal Government and the East Regional Government was now inevitable. It must be said in its favour that the decree itself, which vested legislative and executive powers in the Supreme Military Council, whose decisions on important national matters required *the concurrence of all military governors*, was, to the above extent, directly in line with the *Aburi accord*.

Furthermore on the face of it, the military governor within each region received enough powers to make himself virtually autonomous.

But very reminiscent of General Ironsi's Decree No. 34, it was unfortunately and unnecessarily adulterated by a suspicion-laden addendum which provided that the regional governors should not exercise the powers accorded them in such a way as "to impede or prejudice the authority of the Federation or endanger the continuance of the Federal Government" and that for the declaration of a state of emergency in any region of the federation, the consent of only three of the four governors was required. In normal times such restrictive provisions would have aroused very little interest or suspicion. But the time was far from normal and the slightest act by either of the two parties in dispute was subjected to microscopic scrutiny. It was already clear enough that if the constitution did not openly and expressly allow for secession, it could only be legally achieved as a result of a *unanimous* decision by the Supreme Military Council, especially in view of the earlier provision of the decree that decrees and decisions on matters "affecting or relating to territorial integrity . . . shall come into operation only with the concurrence of the Head of the Federal Military Government and all the Military Governors."

Further emphasis was therefore unnecessary and, considering the highly charged atmosphere at the time, unwisely provocative.

Like General Ironsi's Decree No. 34 it said too much and left nothing to be understood. To the pressure group in Eastern Nigeria it gave an opportune excuse to point to discrimination and threats directed against the East. This slip by the federal authorities was very efficiently exploited by the "secession group" and an appreciation of its impact in the East explains much of "*Ojukwu's intransigence.*" Thus were the various efforts, appreciable in many respects, made by the Federal Government at conciliation in the crucial interval between the Aburi meeting (January 1967) and secession (May 1967) brought to naught by a single but fatal flaw.

Having solemnly promised the whole nation in his address to the Ad Hoc Constitutional Conference on 12th September 1966 that he would not impose a constitution on the people, General Gowon was in honour bound to seek other alternatives to deal with Lt. Col. Ojukwu's "intransigence" than the imposition of a constitution on the whole people of Eastern Nigeria. As long as Lt. Col. Ojukwu was still the military governor, it could not be validly argued that in his stand vis-à-vis the Federal Government, he did not represent all the peoples of the Eastern Region and therefore could be left out of such an important decision, any more than General Gowon himself could justify his own claim, so recently after the July coup, to represent the whole of Nigeria. It was wrong to embark on deciding on a constitution for the people of the East without at least the participation of a legally accredited representative of the people of that region. If the Federal Military Government felt convinced that Lt. Col. Ojukwu was being only personally awkward and that he did not represent the stand of Easterners as a whole, it should have tested this conviction by taking steps to remove him from office and if he resisted by launching its *police action* precisely for that purpose. Such a step would have been more in keeping with enforcing discipline within the army. Imposing a constitution on the people of the Eastern Region after a solemn promise not to do so was a gross political mistake. We have seen and are still seeing its consequences.

For its part, Lt. Col. Ojukwu's East Regional Military Government, whatever may be its justifications for reacting against the Federal Government's "breach of faith" with regard to the *Aburi accord* by choosing secession from among all the alternatives open to it, not only disappointed many Nigerians but unfortunately lost the sympathy of numerous potential supporters of its cause outside the Eastern Region. As a number of informed Easterners warned privately at the time, it has now become clear, especially in the light of its current tragic consequences, that the secession of the Eastern Region at the time and in the manner in which it occurred was a hazardous and costly political decision.

It has not solved the problem that faced the Easterners. It merely inflamed it. If separation were to have come by agreement, as was the case between Malaya and Singapore, between India and Pakistan, between Senegal and Mali, or as was also the case with the former Central African Federation which produced the present Zambia, Rhodesia and Malawi, few people would have had cause to quarrel with it and the present conflict would not have arisen. But such was not the case. It took place in the teeth—now in the armed teeth—of federal opposition.

As many critics of secession have pointed out, the first, and perhaps the most important obstacle in the way of secession, is that the Eastern Region with its population of fourteen million contains probably over five million people belonging to the minority ethnic groups—the Ibibios, Efiks, Ogojas, Ijaws, Ekois, etc. These people are as much opposed to domination by the majority tribe—Ibo—as the Ibos themselves are opposed to domination by the Hausa-Fulani-controlled Northern Region. As long, however, as the federal structure existed, the minorities in each region had safety valves which in case of need assured them access to protection by the Central Government which controlled not only the army and the police but played a big part in initiating economic development in the country. (Indeed, such special acts on the part of the Federal Government as the establishment of the Niger Delta Commission, etc., illustrate the reality of this protection even in the economic field.) Furthermore, the existence of the Federal Parliament whose members did not have to go through the regional bottleneck to get to the centre—but were elected directly to the central parliament by their home constituencies, and were not answerable to the regional governments for their parliamentary activities—was a considerable political guarantee against the oppression of the minorities in each region. This made it possible for them to expose their complaints effectively to the nation at large and to invoke direct federal intervention to accord them redress.

It was, therefore, these guarantees available within the larger framework of the Federation that provided the shock absorber for minority fears and feelings against domination by the majority ethnic group in each region. In the Eastern Region in the past, those minorities who felt the need to do so, preferred to give their political support to the A.G. (Action Group)—an opponent of the N.C.N.C. (National Council for Nigerian Citizens)—which controlled the East Regional Government. In the West (before the creation of the Mid-West), where the Action Group itself was in power, most minority elements there supported the N.C.N.C. Similarly in the North, the Action Group won the support of the minorities of the "Middle Belt" and the N.C.N.C. secured the alliance of N.E.P.U. (Northern Elements Progressive Union)— all in opposition to the N.P.C. (Northern Peoples' Congress), which was the political party in control of the North Regional Government. Indeed, it has been this kind of "cross-threading" which largely reinforced the national fabric and produced a measure of elasticity that kept the country going despite numerous existing ethnic conflicts.

Against the above background of our history, it can be clearly seen that secession was not a solution to the problem of domination. For the minorities of the Eastern Region it shut the safety valves that gave them access to political and economic protection which the larger and more powerful Federation provided them. In this respect, therefore, it can be said that secession only shifted the problem of domination—the very same problem it purported to solve—in favour of the majority tribe—the Ibos—at the expense of the minorities.

Claims that many minorities are fighting with Biafra are true. But equally true is the indisputable fact that many of them are fighting against her. Given the tribal complications of our national politics and the ethnic composition of the Eastern Region such a serious and basic issue as total separation from Nigeria should not depend on anything other than mass approval through a referendum conducted among the minorities whose interests are most affected by separation along the territorial boundaries claimed by Biafra. Biafra has of late rightly proposed a referendum to test opinion in disputed areas. But this proposal, coming only after and not before these areas had been "liberated" by the Federal Government, loses much of its moral force as an act based purely on principle and not on belated political expediency.

A second argument against this style of secession is based on considerations external to the Eastern Region (Biafra) itself. This is the possible adverse repercussions that *separation by force and not by agreement* can have firstly on what would be left of Nigeria and secondly on the African continent as a whole.

Already in Nigeria we have on our hands enough problems raised by the demand being made by various ethnic groups to have their own states within the Federation. Successful secession in any part of the country will in all probability improve the separatist appetite of the leaders of these movements and encourage them to demand full independence for their various peoples.

Provoking such a situation is surely undesirable for numerous reasons. The conflicts that will follow each new attempt to secede will be as painful and as ruinous as the current one.

While it is true, as has been argued by many people, that Nigeria at the beginning of the century was no more than a *geographical expression*, the present conflict has gone a long way to establish the fact that the interval of nearly seven decades has been used to forge, if not the full structure, certainly the frame of a nation. An argument used often, with some justification, to show that Biafrans have demonstrated their will to be a nation and therefore should have a state of their own, is the fact that they have fought so tenaciously to defend their new state. Using this as a yardstick, we will be faced with the sudden realization that the two hundred and twenty-five other ethnic groups which make up the rest of Nigeria have also by their tenacity in the same fight demonstrated their basic unity of purpose—their determination to have one indivisible nation. Like Biafrans, they too are making some sacrifice to this end.

The point which has thus been made clear is that even though Nigeria started off a mere *geographical expression* with artificial boundaries, today there is enough evidence that she has grown the basic roots required of a nation.

It has often been glibly said that Nigeria is not a nation because it is composed of many different ethnic groups. If ethnic homogeneity is the criterion for nationhood then there is no country that qualifies to be a nation anywhere in the world.

What is true of Nigeria as far as ethnic groups are concerned is true of practically every other country in Africa today. Nigeria's neighbours offer abundant examples. The Republic of Dahomey has a partly Yoruba population—the same ethnic group that inhabits Lagos, the whole of Western Nigeria and a part of Northern Nigeria. The Republic of Niger has a partly Hausa population—the majority ethnic group in Northern Nigeria. Northern Ghana has also a considerable Hausa population. The Republic of Chad shares her Kanuri population with Nigeria. The Fulbes (Fulani) in the Cameroun Republic have the exact same ethnic affinity among themselves as they have with those

Fulbes in Adamawa and Sardauna Provinces of Nigeria. Beyond Nigeria's immediate neighbourhood we have the Ivory Coast and Ghana which share the same Baoule tribe—a gifted ethnic group that produced for both countries such distinguished sons of Africa as former President Kwame Nkrumah of Ghana and the respected President Houphouet-Boigny of Ivory Coast. The Republic of Togo shares the Ewes with Ghana. The Fulbes (Fulani) share the Republics of Mali, Guinea, Niger, Senegal and Upper-Volta with other ethnic groups.

It is thus evident that the question of ethnic homogeneity is not vital to the formation of a nation.

What is important is that the different peoples should agree to live together or agree to separate along clearly defined lines.

The peoples of the former Republics of Tanganyika and Zanzibar agreed to live together and so formed the present Republic of Tanzania. The communities of pre-independence India agreed to separate along clearly defined lines and formed the present Republics of India and Pakistan.

In the current Nigerian situation what we have is a stalemate—no definite agreement to live together but no agreement to separate. In such a case only a compromise solution is reasonable and realistic. We should not separate—since there is no agreement to do so—but we should not suffocate ourselves in too tight an embrace—since there is not yet total agreement to cling together. The important thing is that in the light of our past and present experiences, an adjustment should be made such that can allow the best in the different communities to come out while keeping the worst in them in adequate check.

The Nigerian Federal Constitution as it stood at the opening of 1966—that is before the introduction of the current army rule —could be compared in geometrical terms to a rhombus.

Taken in its totality, this particular rectangle has everything that is required to make a square, namely four equal sides and a total angular sum of 360°. Yet it cannot stand squarely on any plane simply because the angles are unevenly distributed. In Nigeria we have nothing to add or subtract in order to make our country firm and stable. The only treatment required is the mere adjustment of the angles of our constitutional rhombus to make them right angles and so produce a structure that can stand squarely on any given national base.

I do not believe that this task is in any way beyond our capabilities.

In view of the reality and peculiar awkwardness of our situation, the time has come for us to try the same trick as Christopher Columbus did some five centuries ago. He made an egg stand on one of its ends, simply by flattening and thus broadening its base. We can make Nigeria stand, and all our people secure and happy, by broadening the base upon which our union is founded. Until our various peoples have had enough time to learn more about one another and discover and appreciate the hidden beauty and values locked up in the multifarious habits and cultures of our numerous ethnic groups, we have no realistic choice open to us other than that of lengthening—and thus relaxing the cracking tension on it—the cord that holds us together.

Herein lies the case for a *loose federation—a United States of Nigeria* based with suitable modifications (such as increasing the number of states beyond the original four and making the desired allowance for a civilian instead of a military regime) on the *Aburi accord.*

NOTES

1. Biafran Ministry of Information, Comp., *The Nigeria-Biafra Conflict* (Papers submitted to the O.A.U. Consultative Committee at Addis Ababa, August 1968), (Biafra, August 1968), pp. 46-47 (This paper had a restricted circulation and was never put on sale).
2. Nabob B. Graham-Douglas, *Ojukwu's Rebellion and World Opinion* (London, Galitzine, Chant, Russell Partners Ltd., 1968).
3. *Africa and the World,* vol. 3, no. 31, May 1967, p. 16.
4. Ibid., p. 16.

5. Ibid., p. 16.
6. *The Meeting of the Nigerian Military Leaders held at Aburi Ghana, 4-5 January 1967*, Official Document No. 5, 1967, no. WT 1000/367/10,000 (Eastern Regional Government publication), p. 7.

CHAPTER 5

A LOOSE FEDERATION OF SIX STATES
FOR TRANSITION PERIOD

The system proposed and promulgated by General Gowon's Federal Military Government—*a federation with twelve states*—has its merits. The principal one is that it tackled effectively the most major obstacle of the *Balewa Federation*, being a direct and courageous attempt to correct the imbalance in the size and weight of the regions that made up the Federation. The second and equally important merit is that by creating new states it has given the *minorities* (the smaller ethnic groups) freer and more direct access to the centre thus securing for them a greater voice there than was permitted by the old federation.

Judged from the angle of these two important achievements the proposed constitution has a good deal to commend it in principle. Indeed, in some other ways and in more auspicious circumstances it might very well have passed with only minor adjustments as suitable for Nigeria.

But there are two sides to the new coin. The reverse side upon close examination reveals two major flaws:

1. The first is that it is a constitution imposed by force without proper consultation by a group enjoying the temporary advantage of superiority in arms. Such a situation is an invitation to trouble and a most unreliable foundation for political stability. Silence and timid acquiescence induced by fear and compulsion

cannot effectively replace the genuine consent of the people as a basis for lasting settlement. Born as it is in a climate of distrust and commotion, it draws its main support from a tenuous and transient unity—unity-in-arms, forged hurriedly in the flames of anti-secessionist fury. This sort of unity has no solid basis or support in the facts of today's bitter but true circumstances of our national life.

The chances are that when the camouflaging dust of confusion clears we will find ourselves face to face with the one basic and unfortunate reality. This is that the prerequisite for national cohesion and therefore stability in a *strong central government*— the integration of our various peoples especially psychologically and emotionally—has not advanced far enough to bear and support the squeezes and strains necessarily demanded by centralized control. A discovery of this fact lay behind the Richards Constitution of 1946, which introduced the idea of regionalisation. An unwise disregard of the same inescapable political reality by General Ironsi (whose Decree No. 34 of 24th May 1966 established strong central control) provoked immediate bitter consequences which ultimately led to his overthrow and death.

The main and, I dare say, fatal weakness of a strong centre in the context of today's Nigeria is that as long as the centre controls too high a proportion of the policy and purse of the entire country, control of power at the centre becomes automatically the attractive target of all those who aim at political or economic power. Simply because our people are, for the time being, largely disparate ethnic groups far too insufficiently welded together, whosoever is in power in Lagos is seen, or can be easily made to be seen, by his opponents as only representing the interests of his own immediate ethnic group. For those outside his own ethnic group, the mere fear of domination by his tribe is enough to engender distrust of whatever he does.

Inversely, once in control at the centre, a leader forced by practical political considerations and especially the realization of the distrust which other tribes could harbour for him comes *ipso facto* under very strong temptation to reinforce his position by appointing to sensitive posts, requiring a high degree of trust and confidence, people upon whose trust and confidence he can absolutely rely. Invariably, many of such people will come from his tribe. They are people whose tribal attachment ensures automatic loyalty to him and whom, in any case, he had the opportunity to know and trust, having grown up with and among them.

In a situation, therefore, where ethnic loyalty is ahead of national loyalty, having a system which directly or indirectly leads in practice to very strong central control is for the time being unrealistic. What is required is an arrangement which first of all guarantees the overall unity of the country but which avoids making the centre too attractive politically and economically to force conflicting interests and ambitions into fierce and unbridled competition to secure control of it. Until better education and the fruits of enlightened and positive leadership will have made our people adequately aware of their common interests and responsibilities at the national level, the desired arrangement is one which will distract just the right amount of attention from the centre by allotting enough powers and responsibilities to the States so as to make them sufficiently attractive for able and talented local men and women to invest their energies in the development of their respective areas, but which at the same time leaves adequate room for genuine and realistic cooperation at the national level.

The argument often produced against such an arrangement is that weakening the control of the central government would lead to ultimate disintegration of the country. In theory this argument is valid. In practice it is hollow. One reassuring fact which the present war itself has brought vividly to light is that the idea of one country has permeated the minds of Nigerians much more than anyone, judging from our constant tribal and political bickerings, would have imagined. You require an ideal to keep over two hundred different ethnic groups fighting together for nearly two years. It is the attempt at secession by the Eastern Region—that is, an attempt to break Nigeria's unity—which has united otherwise bitter enemies to fight a common cause—the cause of one Nigeria. It is therefore clear that while the risk of disintegration exists from a loose federation, this risk is by no means abnormal and is indeed grossly exaggerated. On the contrary, we have already seen samples of the possible consequences of attempts to impose strong central control when the people are unready for the exercise. General Ironsi's Decree No. 34 was opposed by Northern leaders as an attempt to force unity too early. Now that the shoe is on the other foot, Biafrans, accusing General Gowon of going back on the *Aburi accord*, are opposing him largely for the same reason.

Indeed, since the present crisis broke out, whenever our people have had the opportunity to deliberate freely on the form of association required, they have time and again recommended a loose federation. Important parts of the reports submitted by the Northern, Eastern and Lagos-cum-Western delegations to the Ad Hoc Constitutional Conference of September 1966 recommended a loose federation. This was done by the civilians. Nigerian military leaders when they met in Aburi, Ghana, in January 1967 also recommended some form of decentralization. This is to say that whenever the atmosphere permitted genuine deliberation, the necessity for some form of decentralization always came up. This is a significant fact which should not be lightly disregarded. It should indeed be our guide in our search for a balanced form of association between our peoples within the framework of one country.

General Gowon himself, before he became involved in interested pressure from those bent on maintaining a strong centre, had taken a most clearheaded stand when he told the Ad Hoc Constitutional Conference of September-October 1966 that short of breaking up Nigeria or forcing a unitary system of government (which actually means strong central government), the constitutional formula acceptable would include a *federation with a weak centre*, or even an outright *confederation*. I think these were sane ideas developed at a time when the present war fever had not brought confusion into our thinking. They were very realistic ideas then. They are still realistic now. There is no reason to change them.

Because of the small size and evidently limited capacity of many of the states proposed, quite irrespective of any theoretical guarantees that may be inserted in the constitution, the system once in actual operation is bound to lead in fact to strong central control. We have already seen the difficulties and weaknesses inherent in having too strong a centre at the present stage of our national development.

Strong central control can result from two sources: a) a straightforward unitary system or b) a Federal system with a strong centre.

The present twelve-state formula falls undesirably within category (b) above. Some of the states are for the time being just too limited in resources (both in material resources and trained personnel) to ensure the desired degree of independence from the Federal Government.

2. The second flaw in the proposed constitution is that both in concept and in practice the new arrangement is largely a *minorities federation*. The attempt to satisfy minority aspirations, legitimtae as it is, appears nevertheless to have been pushed too far too fast.

The most glaring example of this penchant towards minority considerations is the division of the Eastern Region—Biafra—into three states in which the Ibos with a population of seven to eight million have one state, and the minorities who share between them a population of five million are accorded two. An arrangement which disfavours either group will be unstable. In the interest of sheer stability we should aim at a genuine

73

equilibrium, not a seesaw in which majority and minority group interests take greedy and giddy turns at dominating the country.

For a long time to come and indeed, I dare say, perhaps for always, there is bound to be the question of minorities. In a case such as ours, involving a conglomeration of some two hundred and fifty ethnic groups, this kind of situation is perfectly normal. However, what this means in practical political terms is that minority aspirations can never be totally satisfied until each and every one of the two hundred and fifty groups gets a state of its own. The proper and more meaningful approach to this problem, therefore, is not to attempt to satisfy *ad plenum* these multifarious aspirations. This is impossible in practice. Our aim should rather be to contain these aspirations within a framework which while it allows them a reasonable degree of satisfaction does not go so far as to endanger the delicate stability of the nation as a whole.

It is a platitude to state that where there are competing interests which have of necessity to coexist within one frame, any realistic solution lies in striking the proper balance between the extreme demands of these interests. The twelve-state arrangement is an attempt to strike this balance. But it is only an attempt.

The public statement issued by the government of the Mid-Western state of Nigeria in July 1968 under the title *Understanding the Nigerian Crisis* contains the following comment on the twelve-state formula.

> With the creation of twelve states in Nigeria, the fundamental problem which threatened to dissolve a political association of over fifty years has been solved. It is clear that the States represent a successful attempt to reconcile conflicting interests of the ethnic communities with their desire to participate in the Federal process as one people. The new structure of States will provide the basis for welding together the heterogeneous communities of Nigeria into a nation forging the chain of common values, common culture and sharing a common citizenship and common experience. The internal structure of the new state will curb the excesses of any ethnic group and ensure peace and stability and

provide a wide margin of security for the reoccurrence of the present crisis on such an unprecedented scale in the future. Ibo leaders must give up the plan of leading Nigeria as an ethnic group and contrive new ones of participating in the Federal process as individuals. It is on this basis that they can make a constructive contribution to Nigerian history.[1]

So far as it goes, the above statement very clearly demonstrates the desire of its authors and other like-minded Nigerians to seek and secure lasting settlement to the current crisis—settlement based on fair play and on an equitable adjustment of our constitutional arrangement to accommodate the conflicting interests of those who may desire to dominate on the one hand, and those who are more likely to be dominated on the other. But recognizing a necessary objective is one thing and taking the most effective and realistic means to attain it is another. The attitude reflected in this statement, although well-meaning, is overoptimistic. For example, it describes the twelve-state arrangement as already *a successful attempt to reconcile conflicting interests* when in fact it is right now evident that numerous important interests are actually kicking against it. The current war itself, and the secession of Eastern Nigeria which preceded it, were directly precipitated by the imposition of this very same Twelve-State Constitution. There are signs that certain other important interests in Western Nigeria and Northern Nigeria—interests that cannot be lightly ignored—have not yet accepted the necessity for this particular arrangement. All that can be said with wisdom and modesty is that it is an *attempt to reconcile conflicting interests*. It is premature, if not insincere, to claim that it is already *a successful attempt* in the face of all that is happening at the moment.

The idea that *Ibo leaders must give up the plan of leading Nigeria* is a good one, if such a plan did exist. Similarly, it is necessary that no ethnic group or combination of groups should worm themselves into a position where they can plan to dominate the country successfully. The principle should apply not only to the major ethnic groups—Hausa, Ibo and Yoruba—but to the minority groups as well. What we should strive for is a situation in which neither the majority nor the minority groups are in a position to dominate the entire country. This will necessarily demand an arrangement whose most important function will be just to hold the ring while we grow up and progressively shed our tribal colours and prejudices. Failure to strike such a balance will lead to recurrent instability.

The twelve-state arrangement is clearly as overweighted in favour of minority considerations as the old arrangement of four regions was overweighted in favour of the majority groups.

It is my view that *a federation of six states* would strike a better balance.

Four major considerations should guide any meaningful approach to the creation of states.

1. The pattern of the new states must be conceived on a national rather than a regional basis, thus minimizing our attachment to past prejudices. This means that we should aim as far as possible at destroying the old and baneful concept of the two blocks—*North* and *South*.

The twelve-state arrangement only subdivided the old *North* and the old *South*. This is a failing.

2. While admitting the inevitability of disparity in size and resources, no state should, however, be so dominant as to be able *alone* to dictate to all the others put together. This principle, as we have stated earlier on in this chapter, was thoughtfully and laudably respected by the twelve-state proposal.

3. Each of the states should be in a position—that is, have enough resources—to run its own affairs with tolerable efficiency.

4. Where convenient, and only where convenient, people with the same language, habits and culture should be grouped together. This consideration should not be made a sacred principle nor should it be used as an exclusive guide.

With the above considerations in mind we can then, as a

purely *transitional* arrangement, conceive of a *United States of Nigeria* comprising six states, the whole country being re-arranged as follows:

1. North Western State — Sokoto, Katsina, Kano and Zaria provinces.
Population: 13 million approximately.

2. North Eastern State — Bornu, Bauchi, Adamawa and Sardauna provinces.
Population: 7.6 million approximately.

3. Central State — Niger, Plateau and Benue provinces.
Population: 5.8 million approximately.

4. South Western State — Abeokuta, Ijebu, Ibadan, Oyo, Ondo and Ilorin provinces.
Population: 12 million approximately.

5. South Central State — Delta, Benin and Kabba provinces.
Population 3.6 million approximately.

6. South Eastern State — Onitsha, Rivers, Owerri, Ogoja and Calabar provinces.
Population: 12.8 million approximately.

The Federal Territory — should retain the special status it enjoyed in the old federation but should be expanded to include the former colony province as indeed envisaged by the twelve-state proposal.
Population: 1.2 million approximately.*

I may perhaps have to emphasize here that my recommendation for a *six-state formula* as outlined above is guided principally by considerations of what I believe to be by far our safest course at this period when mutual trust and confidence still

* Population figures based on 1962-1963 census.

require time to recover. It is aimed at securing and preserving the foundation, the four walls and the roof of our national edifice. When the storm is clearly over and the building itself is safe, then we can address ourselves to the second-degree problem of further internal partitioning and other forms of adjustment. My limitation of the number of states to six does not therefore exclude the possibility nor does it deny the desirability of having more states in due and proper time. It is a formula arrived at as a middle-course solution which a) corrects the gross imbalance in the size of the former four regions that made up the old federation, b) gives a measure of satisfaction to the genuine desire of the minorities to have separate states of their own to a point where their worst fear—domination by the majority ethnic groups—is considerably reduced. In respect of the two characteristics above it agrees with and supports the same principle as the twelve-state formula.

The point of divergence is therefore on the number of states. My proposal of six states as against twelve states emanates from the need to limit the number of states *for the time being* to the minimum required to achieve the advantages outlined in (a) and (b) above without making some of the states too weak to cope with the responsibilities which increased local autonomy (that is, reduced dependence on the central government) will of necessity impose on them.

Each of the states in the new federation should be free to choose any name it likes. The former Eastern Region for example if it so desired could retain the name of Biafra. The South-Central state could become the State of Benin if the majority of the people there so prefer. The Central State could become Niger State and so on. The essential point is that we should concentrate our efforts on saving the *substance* of our union. It will also be necessary to envisage and agree that when in future a new state is created it should be the responsibility of the whole country, and not just that of the parent state alone, to provide the bulk of the funds needed to set the newly created state administratively on its feet. This will involve providing money for the basic paraphernalia (administrative buildings, etc.) for the new state capital. The bitter experience of abandonment to its lot to which the Mid-West Region was exposed at its inception in 1962 should not be allowed to plague new states to be created in the future. If the creation of a new state is considered necessary in the country, then it is the duty of the entire country, to whose well-being and general prosperity the people of the proposed state had contributed their share, to see to it that the new state has the means to launch itself properly.

The Eastern Minorities—An Urgent Case

In view, however, of the fact that the political implications of secession and the present war itself have affected the Eastern Region more directly and more heavily than the rest of Nigeria, it will be necessary to treat the divergence of opinion here on the creation of states as a very special case. Secession and the war have not only confused and hardened opinions in this region but have brought in their wake considerable bitterness and hatred among the Eastern population as a whole. The fact that the minorities of the region are themselves sharply divided in the present conflict further complicates the matter.

The following examples illustrate this painful division. The Nigerian Commissioner for Foreign Affairs Dr. Okoi Arikpo, who opposes secession and supports the creation of separate states within Nigeria for the Eastern minorities, is himself an Eastern (Biafran) minority man. But exactly so is his Biafran opposite number Mr. Matthew Mbu, a former Federal Nigerian Minister from Ogoja, who is currently fighting on the Biafran side. There are other important minority civilian personalities split between the Federal Government on the one hand and the

Biafran authorities on the other. On the military plane a comparative situation exists. Biafra's Chief of Staff, Major General Philip Effiong, an Ibibio, is a minority man. His former colleague in the Biafran army, Brigadier George Kurubo, also a minority man, is on the Federal side. Fighting on both sides is a handsome quantity of officers and men of various grades from the eastern minority areas.

The above situation being the case, the truth of the matter is that at the moment it is impossible to say with authority what the *will* of the majority of the Eastern minorities is. Until this will is genuinely ascertained, it seems fair to both groups that the status quo be restored to what it had been before the present conflict and confusion erupted, that is, before the promulgation of the twelve-state decree and before the declaration of secession. Precisely because of this sharp division of Eastern minority opinion, it will be necessary in the interest of stability, first of all to ascertain the extent and exact nature of the desire for a separate state or states. This should be done through a popular referendum as was indeed the case when the Mid-Western Region was created in 1962. Once normalcy returns and minority refugees now squatting under miserable conditions in the Ibo heartland are resettled in their homes, then the appropriate time would have come to carry out the exercise of ascertaining the true wishes of the majority of the people. If a clear decision emerges in favour of the creation of a separate state, an authoritative and unchallengeable case would have thus been made for the creation of an "Eastern Mid-West."

It is necessary that those minority elements who desire the creation of a separate state or states in the Eastern Region should show the wisdom and patience expected of them at this hour of national trial and allow time for this important exercise which should be undertaken as soon as a reasonable degree of normalcy returns. For reasons of maintaining the proper balance in the federation as a whole, it will be preferable to think in terms of creating only one Eastern minority state. The question of minorities within "minority" states will constantly arise all over the country but this is like the question of a recurring decimal.

There would be no end to the creation of states were we to go beyond a certain limit in encouraging a process of cellular fission. Nor should a matter of such cardinal importance as the issue of states be misused by any central government to humour or bribe its supporters.

The general arrangement which I have tried to outline above is conceived as a temporary solution, possibly for a trial period of five years. It is aimed at tackling the most prominent weaknesses of the old federation but reserving the ultimate exercise of seeking the ideal solution until a future date when a greater degree of confidence among our various peoples should have been achieved. Right now we are making a very precarious passage in rough waters and it is clearly not the time to attempt anything that might rock our boat too vigorously.

It is most important that this time we should avoid the same myopia which distorted the vision of the anxious young men of the January coup and led them into the catastrophic error of hurrying to secure a once-and-for-all solution. This coming spring (1969) the people of France will be asked to vote on certain important constitutional changes. (The result of that referendum was a victory for the opposition, forcing President De Gaulle to quit office. [April 1969].) The American constitution has undergone several amendments since 1787. That of Great Britain, with Mr. Wilson's current pressure on the House of Lords, shows that even the oldest of constitutions is subject to continual adjustments. In any case, what appears to be of utmost importance today may become much less so when other surrounding factors change.

Those who are genuinely worried about the dangers of a break-up, should we adopt a loose form of federation, ought to take heart from the fact that once we pull through this civil war as one country their fears in this direction are bound to disappear with time.

The idea of a loose federation should not be taken in isolation from other recommendations which I have made in this book—especially my stress on the need for an executive president as head of the new Federal Republic. If the right person is chosen—a near-certainty in view of my further recommendation for a country-wide election to select this one man—the symbol of oneness which he represents within the country, his prestige abroad as the popularly chosen leader of nearly one-fifth of Africa's population, the attention of the outside world and the determination this will provoke in us to measure up to increasing international challenge —all these factors will force us gradually towards a greater sense of oneness.

The emergence of a truly national figure who owes his position to the manifest will of the entire nation and not to parochial and tribal chauvinism is bound to be a solid bulwark in defence of unity. His position and personality will increasingly neutralize centrifugal tendencies. Once we secure reasonable guarantees for future cohesion we should be content to make an assured, even if modest, national debut on a realistic platform—that of *unity in diversity*.

In our present national agony, *time* is perhaps our greatest friend. We need it to learn to live together in greater harmony. Once the national framework is preserved, as time progresses, like fruit on a tree, our maturity into nationhood will come with the days. If we have the patience and wisdom to groom this tree carefully, given our various and rare endowments both in human and natural resources, the harvest cannot but be a bumper—abundant in quantity and high enough in quality to support the elements of what may well prove Africa's best hope for founding a truly modern state—an entity which not only bears the formal appellation of state, but qualifies in fact as one by modern world standards.

Looking beyond the limited horizon of Nigeria and Biafra's immediate interests, it is easy to see that for the heterogeneous African peoples of today, the struggle for survival is as intra-national as it is international. Viewed from this point, it becomes clear that in the final analysis the Ibos cannot be saved in an Africa that is drowning. Carrying on the fight beyond the present limit after so much bloodshed and destruction is not only to the immediate detriment of both sides but to the ultimate detriment of the cause of Africa's much-needed progress. Africa as a whole is already enough of a burden and a bother to the rest of the world and it is time we start thinking seriously of standing on our own feet.

I believe that the country of Nigeria as we know it has just the right geographical size and the resources—human and material—in about the right quantity and variety, so that given enlightened leadership and proper organization it will give Africa its earliest, if not only opportunity to prove that Africans, like any other people, relying on their own innate ability, can contribute usefully to the pool of world progress and overall prosperity.

A successful experiment which preserves our union in a new and forward-looking *United States of Nigeria* will not only perpetuate for today's Nigerians and Biafrans and for their descendants, the obvious economic and political advantages that come with larger groupings in a world where the struggle for survival is becoming increasingly a contest in which only heavyweights have any serious chance of winning, but could very well become the nucleus of a larger, more prosperous and more powerful union of the African peoples. If we can show by the concrete example of practical success that fifty million people representing some 250 different ethnic groups can, under proper arrangement, live and work together under one banner in fruitful harmony, then we should have made the strongest possible case for a still larger African union. Is it really impossible to save the Ibos and Nigeria as well? Must we sacrifice one for the other?

I am convinced that we can manage to save both. I believe also that to do this should be the goal of any far-seeing Nigerian or Biafran who is as Nigerian or Biafran as he is basically African. Under the right arrangement, Ibos, or any other ethnic group for that matter, can be alive and secure in a Nigeria that is equally alive and secure. The mistakes of one ignorant generation should not be allowed to destroy the heritage and hopes of countless generations to come.

NOTES

1. *Understanding the Nigerian Crisis*, No. GPB 429 (68) /369/20,000 (Benin City, Nigeria, August 1968). Also in *West Africa*, 20 July 1968 and in U.K. Press Gazette, 29 July 1968.

CHAPTER 6

INTERVENTION BY OUTSIDERS
The O.A.U.—Recognition—The Big Powers

I think it is totally unrealistic to treat the present Nigerian problem in isolation from the general problem of Africa today. Indeed, in many ways Nigeria is Africa "writ small." Her present situation is representative of many such conflicts and potential upheavals in Africa. There are ethnic and minority problems all over the continent, be it in Ethiopia, in the Sudan, in the Cameroun, in Kenya or in the Congo. This fact explains to a large extent the caution with which many African heads of states have approached Nigeria's present problem. Many of these leaders have adequately manifested their desire to see this problem settled equitably and quickly but they have at the same time shown their concern for the consequences which any particular type of settlement could provoke elsewhere in Africa. They have time and again indicated the necessity for a settlement which guarantees the Ibos their security but which at the same time does not encourage secessionist tendencies in what remains of Nigeria or elsewhere on the continent.

The following extract from the resolution passed by the last summit conference of African heads of states held in Algiers (September 1968) clearly illustrates this point.

The O. A. U. Conference . . . having taken note of the report of the Consultative Committee on Nigeria launches an appeal to the secessionist leaders to co-operate with the Federal authorities in order to restore peace and unity in Nigeria; recommends to the Federal Military Government of Nigeria, if the above conditions are fulfilled, to proclaim the personal security of all Nigerians without distinction until such time as mutual confidence is restored; launches a fresh appeal to all the parties concerned to co-operate in order to ensure quick transit of humanitarian aid to all those who are in need of it; requests all the member states of the U. N. O. to abstain from every action likely to affect the unity, the territorial integrity and peace of Nigeria . . .[1]

Because this problem which is Nigerian today is potentially African tomorrow, the O.A.U. has a duty to take more positive interest in seeing it resolved quickly. It should shake off some of its current timidity. It is no longer enough for it to limit itself to resolutions and pious declarations regarding the need for settlement. After over twenty months of confusion and bloodshed on a scale unprecedented in the history of modern Africa, there is now enough reason for it to act more positively and, as an honest broker, to make concrete proposals for settlement for the consideration of both sides.

Due to the fact that many of our countries in Africa are recent creations in their present form as states, there are still important adjustments to be made within them in order to strike the desired equilibrium between the various ethnic and cultural elements that make up their population. In this kind of situation and in the larger interests of Africa and African peoples, to lend an active hand in settling disputes that arise, especially when such disputes lead to large scale bloodshed, cannot be correctly considered as interference. A neighbour has not only a right but a duty to seek definite settlement to confusion and commotion in the home next door to his own, if the conflict in that home reaches a proportion where murder and arson become evident and the resultant conflagration threatens to spill over into his own house. In such circumstances he will be shirking his duty both to that neighbour and to himself if he just looks passively on, clinging to the theory of noninterference in his neighbor's private affair. A private business that develops into a public nuisance ceases to be a private affair.

It is indeed time for the O.A.U. to abandon its present posture which gives it the occasional and misleading appearance of being the affair of heads of states—preoccupied almost to the point of obsession with the idea of not hurting one another's feelings—as distinct from the affair of the masses of the African peoples themselves. It was largely this attitude of unrealistic detachment which, despite the timely warnings and pleas from countries like Tanzania and Zambia, made the previous O.A.U. Heads of States Conference held in Kinshasa (September 1967) treat the Nigerian conflict as a matter of minor importance. The Consultative Committee which it subsequently appointed to examine the issue visited Lagos and, suffering from the same malady, was so concerned with not offending the authorities there that it avoided going to the Eastern Region. It wrote its report and gave its judgment without hearing the "rebel" side. After such an unfortunate neglect of its duty to Africa—a neglect that has already forced a bitter division among African countries—it is now faced with the onerous task of putting out an unprecedented conflagration. An African organization should take much more determined interest than outside powers in bringing about timely settlement in African disputes and it should intervene early enough and actively enough in such matters to prevent dangerous explosions. To be in a position to do so is the *raison d'être* of the O.A.U.— otherwise Africa has no need for an expensive replica of the United Nations.

Recognition

It is appropriate here to discuss the recognition of Biafra by a number of African states, namely, Tanzania (13th April 1968),

Gabon (8th May 1968), Ivory Coast (14th May 1968), Zambia (20th May 1968).

Below is an extract from the statement made by President Felix Houphouet-Boigny of Ivory Coast showing the reasons that pushed him to recognize Biafra.

> I am today proclaiming my indignation in the face of the inexplicable indifference, the culpable indifference of the whole world towards the massacres that have taken place in Biafra for more than ten months. I am returning to my country distressed, outraged, upset and revolting against the prolongation of this atrocious war. Is it known that there have been more deaths in Biafra within ten months than in Vietnam in three years? This being the case, the problem between the Federation of Nigeria and Biafra must be seen in its true perspective. It is a human problem and a human solution must be found to it. Considerations of peace should take precedence over everything else. If our brothers involved in this conflict cannot live together in a Federation, then let them accept to live in peace as neighbours.[2]

President Houphouet-Boigny's statement was made in Paris on the 9th of May 1968 on his way home to Abidjan where less than a week later his foreign minister formally announced Ivory Coast's recognition of Biafra. The reasons given by the government of the Ivory Coast for taking this important step not only reflected those given earlier by Tanzania and Gabon but were faithfully echoed in the subsequent recognition statement issued by Zambia. One important fact was clearly underlined in all these statements. This is that the recognition of Biafra as an independent state came from the countries concerned principally as a reaction to their disappointment and frustration at the failure of the Federal Nigerian Military Government to respond to appeals to try to settle the conflict otherwise than by force of arms. It was not an approval of the political choice of Eastern Nigeria to secede. This is made clear by the fact that the first recognition did not come until a full ten months after secession.

It was the magnitude of the war and the enormity of the suffering it produced that made the people and leaders in these countries revolt against the method adopted by the Federal Military Government to solve the problem. It is important that all sections in Nigeria including Biafra recognize this fact. Nigerians will be mistaken if they persist in the hostile belief that the countries which recognized Biafra did so in order to embarrass or break Nigeria. There is evidence that the leaders of these countries have shown much greater concern about what is happening to Nigeria and Nigerians than many of our own leaders. Similarly, the leaders of Biafra should understand that the sympathy which compelled these countries to give them recognition was provoked by the suffering of the ordinary people whom the Biafran leadership, despite earlier assurances, proved unable to protect and that the act of recognition was not a premeditated approval of the political choice of secession. Like the secession itself, it was more a *reaction against* than a *decision for*.

Another important aspect of the developments that led to recognition is the revelation that many African leaders, who are generally accustomed to handling the affairs of relatively small and simpler communities, are perhaps not quite in a position to appreciate the complexity of politics in such a large yet inadequately organized community as Nigeria. Intelligent and well-meaning, but lacking the background and insight which the volume and peculiar complexity of the Nigerian situation necessarily demand, they are often exposed to the danger of oversimplifying our problem. It is a lamentable irony that rather than bring the war to an end and so terminate the sufferings of the Biafran masses, recognition provoked an intensification of both. Like most acts born of reaction it produced unexpected counterreactions. Not only did it encourage the hawks on the Biafran side to unnecessary intransigence as far as peace negotiations are concerned, it also provoked in the Federal Military Government an increased determination to make nonsense by military means of whatever gains Biafra may have scored diplomatically.

The Big Powers

The interest shown by the Big Powers and certain countries outside Africa has been subject to conflicting interpretations. This interest falls into a sharply different category from that shown by African states. It goes without saying that now in cold war days as in former colonial days, the underlying motivation behind the attitude of the bigger powers towards Africa and African problems—that is the attitude of the governments of these countries as distinct from that of their populations, whose reactions and sympathy generally emanate from humanitarian considerations—is their own self-interest. It is against this background that foreign intervention in Nigeria must be seen.

These same interests clashed heavily for supremacy in the Congo during the Katanga episode. The Nigerian conflict has now provided them with a handsome opportunity for a return match. The tragedy of the situation however, is that this match is being played in our home and at our expense.

Bearing the above clearly in mind as a general background we can nevertheless attempt an analysis of the more immediate stimuli which provoked each individual country to intervene at the time and in the measure in which it did.

It has been commonly said, and with justification, that British intervention in the Nigerian civil war has been dictated by essentially economic interests. Few people will deny that this is so. Economic interests dictated her intervention in principle, but they do not explain the manner and the measure in which it has come. Britain "split" colonial India before quitting her but continued to maintain practically unabated economic ties with both India and Pakistan after that event. Much the same situation applies to her relations with Malaya and Singapore after the dissolution of the Malayan Federation. But for the important political complications introduced by acute racial disagreement,

Britain would in all probability have continued to maintain harmonious economic ties with the three members of her former Central African Federation—Zambia, Malawi and Rhodesia. The point being made here is that economic interests by themselves need not have forced the hand of normally cautious Britain to take sides with Lagos and to supply arms to her for the destruction of Biafran lives and property. Indeed, with the considerable investment of British firms in oil-rich Eastern Nigeria (Biafra), Britain had every interest in seeking to avoid prolonged civil commotion or destruction in any form. To do so was directly in her economic interest. Politically the Rhodesian sore is also there to argue against her active participation in the use of force.

The cause of Britain's present commitment can be more easily traced to poor political judgment—a faulty appreciation of the prewar situation in Nigeria. The superficiality of British understanding of Nigerian politics and political emotions was first demonstrated by the near-total surprise with which Britain and her representatives in Nigeria received the military coup of January 1966, even though most sensitive Nigerian observers knew that beneath the surface calm of the "model colony," the more enlightened and more active section of the population was seething with ominous discontent.

Again after the counter-coup of July 1966, and especially after the massacres of September-October of that year, British representatives were still unable to fathom the depth of Ibo discontent, and therefore Ibo will and potential strength to resist the Federal Government. It would appear they believed the light-hearted boast which Lt. Col. Hassan Katsina made in early 1967 when he was still military governor of Northern Nigeria that "once the green light was given, federal forces needed only 48 hours to crush the resistance of Eastern Nigeria." Apparently believing in a quick federal victory in the event of an armed clash, Britain saw no point in taking the risk of annoying the federal authorities by preaching compromise and trying if need be to help secure the basic terms of the *Aburi accord* which gave the regions increased political and military autonomy.

It was not until the war itself broke out and Biafran forces not only held their own against federal onslaught but actually overran the Mid-West State and were advancing on Lagos itself that their underestimation of Biafran capabilities awakened the British government to the grave realities of the situation. Having earlier openly declared its support for Lagos in the belief that it would not be called upon to contribute militarily in any substantial way to the military campaign itself, she was now faced with the unhappy choice of honouring her pledge and standing by the Federal Government in a more material way or running the risk of losing Nigeria's friendship to foreign competitors only too anxious to pick up whatever crumbs might fall from Britain's privileged table. In this dilemma, the more radical elements in Nigeria forced Britain's hands. They made overtures to Russia and received a prompt response in military hardware. Britain from this moment on had no choice but to try to compete in order to drive the Russians out of Nigeria. The only way to do so was to give Nigeria what she needed to crush "Ojukwu's rebellion."

British economic interests are not in themselves incompatible with the existence of more than one independent state were Nigeria to break up, as has been clearly demonstrated by the precedents mentioned above in the case of India and Pakistan, Malaya and Singapore, and the former Central African Federation. Indeed, anyone who is familiar with the trend of negotiations for Nigeria's independence will appreciate the depth of feeling in the country—especially in the South—during the hectic last few years of colonial rule, when the British government was openly and frequently accused of plotting to "Pakistanize" Nigeria before giving her independence. The fact that the two Southern regions—East and West—achieved autonomous status (1957) two years before the Northern Region was considered ripe for the same is readily attributable to Britain's attempt to employ delaying tactics to frustrate the Southern politicians and, considering their hurry, to tempt them into asking for independence without the North.

The problem in the Nigerian context is that the present situation presents a dilemma comparable in certain respects to that of the two Chinas. You have to choose one or the other. If Britain cannot keep both Nigeria and Biafra, it is in her interest to strengthen her hold on the bigger of the two and hope through this to secure a "reconquest" of the smaller portion in order to regain the original whole. Neither hatred for the Ibos nor a sacred attachment to the principle of preserving one Nigeria dictated Britain's present position and commitment. Expediency did.

Another power which is supporting the Federal Government in a very substantial way is, of course, the Soviet Union. As a superpower, her interests in today's cold war conflict are primarily political and only remotely economic. Her method is Machiavellian. A latecomer in twentieth century Africa, her motivations are similar to those which propelled the colonial aspirations of Bismarck's Germany in the last century—*to have a place in the sun*. Having burned her fingers and early hopes successively in Guinea and Ghana, she saw the Nigerian situation as a fresh and tempting opportunity to secure a much-needed bridgehead in West Africa. In the Congo, Russia had opposed United Nations' efforts to use force to unify the country; in Nigeria she is supplying the fuel for force.

On the Biafran side two countries stand out prominently for the support and sympathy which they have shown for the Biafran cause: These are France and Portugal. Portugal's reason is not hard to see. It is not entirely humanitarian since her attitude to the fight for freedom by her African colonies puts in doubt any deep respect on her part for the principle of self-determination by African peoples.

Perhaps more interesting and more complicated is the attitude of France. The first official statement from the French government indicating sympathy for the Biafran people came on 31st July 1968, when the Minister of Information, M. Joel Le Theule made the following statement after a cabinet meeting:

> The French Government notes that the bloodshed and sufferings endured for over a year by the population of Biafra have demonstrated their will to affirm themselves as a people . . .
> . . . Faithful to its principles, the French Government considers that as a result, the present conflict should be resolved on the basis of the right of a people to self-determination involving setting in motion the appropriate international procedure to this end.[3]

On the 9th of September, President De Gaulle himself spoke in the following terms:

> . . . In this matter France has aided and aids Biafra within possible limits. She has not taken steps to accomplish the final decisive act—the recognition of the Biafran Republic—because she considers that the matter is above all the affair of Africans. Already there are states both from East and West Africa which have recognized Biafra. Others may perhaps follow. This is to say that for France the decision which has not yet been taken is not excluded for the future and one can indeed imagine that the federation itself, realizing the impossibility of remaining as constituted at its inception, may become transformed into a form of union or confederation which could reconcile the right of Biafra to self-determination with her connections with the whole of Nigeria.[4]

Naturally this obvious inclination towards Biafra has raised an enormous amount of speculation as to French intentions and interests in Nigeria.

Having been in Paris since May 1966 when Nigeria resumed diplomatic relations with France after a six-year break (I was Nigeria's first chargé d'affaires in France) and having followed developments also as Biafra's representative until my resignation last December, I can perhaps claim some knowledge of what happened in France regarding the evolution of French thinking vis-à-vis the Nigerian crisis. Below are quotations from the *Sunday Times* of London and *Le Monde* of Paris, offering explanations for the French attitude to the conflict.

. . . French supplies of arms and ammunition have sharply boosted the collapsing Ibo rebellion against the Nigerian Federal Government. This last-minute infusion for Col. Ojukwu is a tragedy for Nigeria. It merely prolongs the agony and ensures yet more bloodletting in a cause which is indubitably lost. It is not hard to discern French motives for wanting the war to linger on. The war devitalizes a vast and potentially very rich Commonwealth country which happens to be surrounded by far weaker and smaller francophone states. The intervention is at least in part a transference of France's European complexes on to the helpless back of dying Africans.[5]

. . . France which nevertheless recognizes only the Government of Lagos is progressively increasing her aid to Biafra. The French Government considers indeed that Biafrans have acquired the right to self-determination through their sacrifices on the battlefield and the massacres to which Ibos have been subjected. Furthermore, it is felt in Paris that the process of separation has become practically irreversible owing to hatred born of this conflict and that the Nigerian Federation has in any case come to an end.

The French Government emphasizes the humanitarian aspect of its involvement. But it is clear that political considerations have equally dictated its attitude. The Nigerian Federation as it stood in 1966, by the very fact of its size and economic power constitutes a pole of attraction in the gulf of Benin. In the long run this situation could prove prejudicial to the political equilibrium of the whole of West Africa.

It is to be noted that the only French-speaking African countries which have recognized Biafra are Gabon and Ivory Coast, states whose leaders have opposed the maintenance respectively of the former Federation of French West Africa and the former Federation of French Equatorial Africa.[6]

I will not attempt to contradict these important sources but while not doing so, it is only fair to examine France's attitude not only from her current declarations of open support for the Biafran people's rights to self-determination but also from her posture of strict and cold correctness at the beginning of the conflict.

When the political disagreement between the Federal Military Government and East Regional Government began to show signs of an impending military clash, the French government declared an embargo on the exportation of arms to Nigeria including the Eastern Region (Biafra). Indeed certain orders which had been placed by the Federal Government for armoured cars were cut down and delivery was limited to barely one-third of the original order, this fraction representing the portion of the order that was already embarked for shipment. Requests by the Federal Government for the purchase of two dozen French Fouga Magisters and bombs were refused. Even stricter control was applied to the Eastern Region which had to do its clandestine shopping outside of France.

A number of French-built helicopters used by Biafra at the beginning of the war were bought as civilian machines by companies operating in Eastern Nigeria well before the inevitability of a war became apparent. The two American-built B-26 bombers featured on the Biafran side at the beginning of the war were bought in France but through third parties to whom they had been sold for aerial survey purposes and exportation licences obtained months before the conflict developed. To any one who was close to the scene, it was clear that France was meticulously careful not only to avoid being drawn into the conflict but to discourage the build up of arms and armaments in any part of Nigeria. The key to French "intervention" on the Biafran side is to be found firstly in French public opinion and intense pro-Biafran sentiment, and secondly in the involvement of respected African leaders on the Biafran side. Very early in the struggle Biafran propaganda saw to it that documents were printed in French and made readily available to important sections of French public opinion. The press was briefed fully on every development and French journalists were encouraged to go to Biafra and report to their people what they saw. It was largely the capture of French public opinion that laid the foundation for the French government's open identification with the struggle of the Biafran people. Letters were addressed by constituents to their representatives in parliament, including cabinet ministers, the then Foreign Minister, M. Couve de Murville, and the then Prime Minister, M. Pompidou himself, urging them all for action in favour of Biafra. These pressures could not remain without effect, especially at a time when the heads of states of certain African countries like the Ivory Coast and Tanzania began to show their impatience with the attitude of Lagos and to manifest their support for the Biafrans.

It has been suggested that French African countries, namely, Ivory Coast and Gabon, were instigated by France to act in the way in which they did. This is not correct. The contrary, in fact, happens to be the case. Ivory Coast and Gabon are not the only African countries where France has influence. As a matter of fact these two being among the richest can afford as much independence from French official line on foreign policy matters as the rest of O.C.A.M. (Afro-Malagasy Common Organization) members. On such important international issues like the attitude to the People's Republic of China or the Middle-East crisis, France and the Ivory Coast have constantly disagreed. So too with Gabon. The truth of the matter is that both President Houphouet-Boigny and President Bongo have little faith in the cohesive force of federations. Their past political records help to illustrate this fact. It was President Houphouet-Boigny who actually successfully led the opposition to France's programme for a French West African Federation and insisted on independence for each individual state. Gabon also was the first to pull out of the Federation of French Equatorial Africa.

With this basic attitude it was easy for both leaders to see the inevitability of failure in the Nigerian federal experiment. When

97

war erupted and bloodshed and destruction mounted as the war progressed, they felt their instincts had been vindicated.

Indeed, French officials made no secret of their intention to keep clear of the struggle which they regarded essentially as an African affair. The breakthrough which Biafra achieved with both President Houphouet-Boigny of Ivory Coast and President Nyerere of Tanzania was the one factor that altered the situation. Not only did it encourage the impression that serious, thinking Africans were now on Biafra's side, the case of President Houphouet-Boigny in particular, who is greatly respected in France, literally obliged the French government to take a more serious and positive decision in line with the attitude and stand of President Houphouet-Boigny himself. The involvement of France came therefore as a result of presures exerted on her by respected African leaders and by French public opinion at home.

There is no doubt that as a big power France had her own political interests in mind. However, her immediate economic stakes in that area, like those of Britain, are spread all through Nigeria and Biafra. Her support for Biafra came at a time when practically all important assets in the Eastern Region had fallen into federal hands, and even this support has not been on a scale or of the character than can ensure Biafra's total independence from Lagos. It began as a reluctant support demanded and pressured by respectable African leaders. It still appears aimed at saving the Ibos from total destruction but not making them strong enough to challenge Nigeria as effectively as total independence would demand. Diplomatically, France still maintains her relations with the Federal Government of Nigeria.

However, it will be a waste of time and energy to concentrate our attention on blaming outsiders for taking advantage of the opportunity we ourselves offered them.

Such a negative attitude will solve nothing. These powers know what they are doing. They know their own interests. The important question that should occupy our minds right now is whether we can say that we know what we are doing, whether we know our own true interests.

When tragedy befell the country in 1966 not even our unprecedented refugee problems attracted more than passing attention. But this apathy was not universal. The refugee problem that resulted from the Middle-East upheaval of the same period, even though it affected less than a quarter of the number involved in Eastern Nigeria alone, provoked not only immediate sympathy but generous material aid from these same powers.

Furthermore, before the present conflict developed, important national projects such as the Kianji Dam, the iron and steel industry planned for the country and, indeed, similar other projects of vital importance to a developing country, were able to attract only the most sluggish support from outside, despite their known advantages to the country. But within only a few months of fighting, foreign aid began to pour in—foreign destructive aid with which to destroy our own people. Is this not enough to make any serious Nigerian stop and think? It is amazing how swiftly we have become credit-worthy when we are up in arms against one another for the destruction of our own lives, our own property and our common economy. What is this foreign aid really worth? What does it mean to those who are giving it? Where it comes as a gift, our generous donors are actually spending only a tiny percentage of their immense stock. Where, as is mostly the case, we purchase, their arms production is, to the extent of the supply given to us, being encouraged.

Now at war we have begun once again to drift just as we did in pre-war politics. We are fighting a war which is being fed by outsiders, who have strings attached to the arms they supply. Sooner or later, their permeation amongst us will begin to have effect. These powers will want to direct our policies.

Let us brace ourselves while we have have the time to do so to put an end to the internalization of our quarrel. The moment is fast approaching when we shall find ourselves unable to halt the ominous international momentum, the build up of which our folly is steadily encouraging. Drifting is bad enough in ordinary peace-time politics. In war it is catastrophic.

NOTES

1. "Resolution sur le Nigéria du Sommet de l'O.U.A. Algers, September 1968," *A.F.P. Bulletin quotidien d'Afrique,* 16 September 1968, [Author's transl.].
2. *Le Monde* (Paris), 10 May 1968, [Author's transl.].
3. "Biafra," *A.F.P. Bulletin Conseil des Ministres,* 31 July 1969, [Author's transl.].
4. "Afrique Occidentale–Nigéria; De Gaulle et le Biafra," *A.F.P. Bulletin quotidien d'Afrique,* no. 6687, 10 September 1968, [Author's transl].
5. *Sunday Times* (London), 6 October 1968.
6. *Le Monde* (Paris), 1 November 1968, [Author's transl.].

CHAPTER 7

THE ARMY AND THE NATION

The Armed Forces—Size and Structure

On the eve of the first coup d'etat (January 1966) Nigeria with her 55 million people had an army of under 9,000 men! At this time, already fully Nigerianized, it had at its head the most senior officer—Major General Aguiyi-Ironsi (an Ibo from the East). Next to him were Brigadier Ademulegun (a Yoruba from the West), Brigadier Maimalari (a Kanuri from the North) and Brigadier Ogundipe (a Yoruba from the West).

As of today, after the heavy toll of two coups d'etat and a raging war, only the last named is alive. Having been spared by the January coup (he was away from Nigeria when it took place) and narrowly escaping death during the July counter-coup (he fled pistol in hand from his northern body guards and sought sanctuary aboard the navy's frigate), he was glad to quit the army for a distant post abroad as Nigeria's High Commissioner to the United Kingdom.

Below these "big four" were some 350 officers made up of a few colonels, an inflated number of ubiquitous Lt. Colonels, then majors, etc., drawn fairly evenly from the various regions but perhaps with more Ibos than any other ethnic group represented. The ranks were dominated by Northerners who were mainly G.D.'s—general grades. They did the shooting. The Southerners—Yorubas, Ibos, Efiks, Edos, etc.—took more easily to the technical and clerical jobs. This division of labour was to prove crucial when the army's unity broke under the impact of the two coups. Dominating the officer class, the Southerners, especially the Ibos, had found it easy to plot the January coup and used troops under their command to execute unlawful orders.

When the Northern sector rallied after the shock, although inferior in numerical officer strength—an inferiority accentuated by the recent elimination of its most promising officers—it nevertheless consisted of enough fighting men not only to pose a serious threat to the Eastern Region but in Chief Awolowo's own words, to keep the Western Region as well in "effective occupation."

The Nigerian air force, only just formally constituted, had some twelve trainer aircrafts and a handful of instructors recruited from West Germany. This fact helps to explain its conspicuous absence in the early days of the war. Nigeria's entire navy consisted of its flagship—N.N.S. Nigeria—a Dutch-built frigate and four smaller patrol vessels. At its head was a Nigerian, Commodore Wey, who survived the two coups and still as Head of the Navy is the oldest, and very much respected, member of Nigeria's Supreme Military Council.

Nigeria's police force was organized at two levels: *a*) the *Nigeria police*—that is, the federal police; *b*) the *local government police*, which came directly under the control of the regional governments.

Altogether they numbered some 24,000. However only the Northern and Western regions had any effectively established local government police forces. The East and Mid-West were content to rely on the Nigeria police units stationed in their regions. Since the Federal Government had overall responsibility for security throughout the country, it had powers in time of need to requisition the local government police forces which in such cases had to take orders directly from the Nigeria police.

An interesting arrangement with regard to the federally-controlled Nigeria police itself is that unified as it was in command at the national level, it was nevertheless organized on an essentially regional basis. For purposes of recruitment and training there were two police colleges—the Southern Police College at Ikeja (near Lagos) and the Northern Police College in Kaduna.

Each of the four regions and Lagos had a commissioner in charge of the Nigeria police units in that region. The coordinating and unifying factor was the National Police Council on which the Regions and Lagos were suitably represented. At the apex of this pyramid and representing the symbol of its unified authority was the Inspector General.

At the time of the January coup, the incumbent was a Northerner—Mr. Kam Salem. His predecessor, who was the first indigenous officer to hold that office, was an Easterner—Mr. Edet.

The Army—Reorganization Needed

With regard to its organization, as outlined above, an arrangement which in no way impaired its efficiency or its reputation as a national institution, the Nigeria police was more realistic than the Nigerian army. It was able to combine regional freedom in routine administration with genuine and effective central control in matters involving policy and operations. This allowance reduced the risks of internal friction which a higher degree of central control was bound to provoke. The Nigerian army, which was really a residual unit of the defunct British West African Frontier Force, had by January 1966 not had enough time to adjust to strictly Nigerian conditions. Nor did it have the problem of size to make it feel the necessity for copying the example set by the Nigeria police. My suggestions below recommending a police-style decentralization are based principally on the fact that quite apart from the urgent, even if temporary, dictates emanating from the hatred and mistrust caused by the war, our army is no more the small unit it used to be.

It has become larger. It will become larger still. Too tight a central control in routine matters can only increase the chances of annoyances and dissatisfaction within the army in a country whose people are still inadequately integrated.

The important question of the army should be approached cautiously and from two angles: *a*) a short term view which should concentrate on what is practical today in our present circumstances; and *b*) a long term view which should aim at what is ideal for the country when normalcy returns.

With the above terms clear in our minds, we should agree on the necessity for retaining as in the old Federation one indivisible army. However, because feelings have yet to cool and confidence has yet to be restored before men bearing arms can begin to mix freely once more, the army should be organized on a state basis for matters concerning recruitment and routine administration. Each of such units should be called an *Area Command*—as was agreed at Aburi.

To ensure effective coordination and control it should be under the overall direction of a National Military Council whose membership should comprise an equal number of representatives drawn from among the most senior officers of each Area Command.

All rules and regulations affecting basic issues such as training and equipment should be the sole responsibility of the National Military Council. So also should be such matters as discipline, promotions and transfers of senior officers within each Area Command. On these subjects Area Commanders should only make recommendations for the consideration of the National Military Council. Each Area Command should be headed by an officer not below the rank of a Major General, who should automatically be the chief representative of his Area Command on the National Military Council.

The chairmanship of the National Military Council should be rotating and should change hands between Area Commands every six months. Decisions by the Council should be by simple majority with each member voting for himself.

The principle of free vote for each member of the National Military Council is of cardinal importance in my present recommendation regarding decentralization. It ensures that, even though membership of the Council is on a state basis as far as representation is concerned, decisions of the Council have a clear possibility of being national. Once selected to represent his state, each officer has the freedom to judge and make his own decisions on the merits of issues that come up before the Council. There is no state "whip" to tell him how to vote. The fundamental advantage in such an arrangement is that, by giving the states equal representation and therefore equal participation, no state enjoys any special advantage nor starts off with any particular handicap. We have now seen clearly enough the importance of the army not just as a war machine but in the decisive role it can play in the political life of the nation. It will be an error to allow any one group to monopolize the armed forces or to dominate it in any shape or form.

Such an arrangement no doubt is likely to run against the conventional idea of indivisibility of authority in the army. Where the danger of monopoly exists, only "collective indivisibility" can ensure fairness. It is clear that in different circumstances a monolithic arrangement would lend itself to easier acceptance. But that was precisely the arrangement which we had up till January 1966 and which failed simply because it was not related adequately to the peculiarities of our national situation. Earlier in this book I have deliberately included quotations from reported details of what happened within the army during the two coups—January and July 1966. These ugly events make it abundantly clear that the army has not progressed more than the population at large away from sectionalism. Much as we regret this reality we would be foolish to ignore it in formulating any serious policy for the future. It is a fact we just have to learn to live with and accommodate until we are able to outgrow it.

The control of the armed forces should be vested in an executive president who should have powers to direct the National Military Council on all matters and to mobilize the entirety of the national armed forces in the case of emergency whether this emergency results from an external or an internal threat to the security or integrity of the state. He should have the title of Commander in Chief of the armed forces in his capacity as Head of State.

This arrangement is conceived as a temporary one in accordance with the short term view of our problem. It should be reviewed as soon as adequate signs of normalcy become evident with a view to encouraging greater integration of the various units. With time there should be no difficulty in switching Area Commanders and recruiting on a national rather than state basis.

The essential thing is that although the long term plan has of necessity to aim at a monolithic and solidly integrated national army, we must not try to achieve this military goal by a forced march. Viewed politically the army is merely a section of the population in uniform. It is subject to the same sentiments and emotions as the population at large. Its integration therefore cannot truly precede the integration of the population itself.

The Navy and the Air Force

However, because of the nature of their organization and mode of operation the case of the navy and the air force must be treated differently.

Respectively aquatic and aerial, the navy and the air force

command a presence among the population very considerably smaller than that of the land forces—army and police.

In the Nigerian context this presence is further diminished by the fact that in relation to the army or police both are still embryo institutions. This means that the problem of size (in this case I mean strictly number of persons involved) is likely to remain relatively small and unimportant in the next few years.

In the period immediately after the war the navy and the air force will have very little need to be active. They should be positively immobilized during the "cooling off" period while negotiations, consultations on a new constitution, rehabilitation activities, etc., are going on. They should be reactivated at the earliest sign of return to normal life, with its attendant reestablishment of mutual confidence.

It is as unrealistic as it is impracticable to think in terms of organizing the navy or the air force, like the land forces, on a state basis. These two sectors of the armed forces therefore should remain as before—on a national basis adjusted, perhaps, to admit a quota system.

Compulsory Military Service

The events of the last three years should by now have brought home to us the necessity for bridging the gap between the mentality of the civil population on the one hand and that of the military on the other. It was largely the disparity between the reactions of the two bodies to the concept of political discipline that provoked the current bloody crisis. As we can neither afford to make every citizen a professional soldier so as to abolish civilian laxity nor disband the army to eliminate their often too rigid concept of discipline, we have interest in settling for a middle course—the introduction of *compulsory military service*.

A national programme should be launched to give military training for a given period to Nigerian citizens—possibly to all males between the ages of eighteen and forty, and all unmarried females between the ages of eighteen and twenty-five. As this section of the population represents the most active stratum, sufficient infusion of military discipline will ensure that the most important portion of the working population understands what the word *duty* means.

On the political plane still greater dividends can be expected. The first result is that the dangerous gap between the mentality of the professional soldier and his civilian counterpart could thus be effectively bridged. The second is that giving military training to practically all able-bodied citizens automatically reduces, if not eliminates, the monopoly of the knowledge of the use of arms otherwise enjoyed by professional soldiers alone. The diminution of this monopoly will reduce the liberty and temptation on the part of the soldier to use force to take over the government. His chances of imposing his will by force or threat of force will then depend on what proportion of the population shares his views. If he does not represent the popular opinion, then there will be enough young men and women who can speak his language and oppose him in arms.

A third and obvious advantage in giving military training to the population at large is the purely military one. It reduces the expensive necessity of maintaining a large standing army for most of the time in lucrative idleness. One good by-product of the present war is that it has opened our eyes to our national military capabilities. Before the war the entire Federation of Nigeria had an army of under ten thousand men. Now between them and under the heavy stress of war, both Nigeria and Biafra are maintaining an army of some one hundred and fifty thousand men. Given our population, with the proper organization and direction, the introduction of compulsory military service can easily ensure in time of need a large body of men and women trained, able and ready to defend their nation.

* * *

I am taking advantage of this revised edition to expound a little on my arguments in support of a certain decentralization of the army somewhat along the lines of the Nigerian police organization. I have heard it said ever since the original edition came out that my suggestions in this regard will weaken the authority of the central government and diminish the cohesive force of the nation. There is definitely some logic, but perhaps more logic than good sense, in this assertion. A monolithic army is obviously the conventional thing. In Nigeria, and especially in our present circumstances, we do not have to be conventional merely for the sake of conforming with tradition. Nigeria's problem is a familiar problem in Africa. It is to find a way for the various ethnic groups, brought together by the accident of colonization to form a modern state, to live together in harmony. Although certain similarities exist between our situation and those that have occurred elsewhere, there is no ready-made example that exactly fits our circumstances.

I have had occasion to recall in another part of this book General Gowon's appreciation of this fact when, in addressing the Ad Hoc Constitutional Conference on 12 September 1966 on the need to find a formula that suited Nigeria's particular circumstances, he spoke of "an entirely new arrangement which will be peculiar to Nigeria and which has not yet found its way into any political dictionary."

Reorganization of the army on the pattern that I have outlined in this chapter has an important political advantage. It should ensure that within the country, the President, as the Head of the Executive, cannot easily abuse his control of the armed forces by employing them for his own limited personal political ends.

He will hesitate to risk his authority in ordering a suitably de-centralized army to take measures that are not in the overall national interest. In internal politics, therefore, his role will become, in practice as well as in theory, that of an umpire, interfering only when the need truly arises. This practical limitation on his freedom to exploit his constitutional control over the army does not in any way amount to weakening the position of the President. Such a definition of his role is actually a political advantage both to himself and the nation at large. The limitation on his freedom to interfere with the army is equally a limitation of his temptation to abuse his power. The less tempted he is to do so, the greater the chances of political stability in the country.

When, however, a real need arises for his intervention, the President's real strength emerges. His vast constitutional authority, including the powers to direct the National Military Council on all matters and to mobilize the entire national armed forces whenever there is a threat to the security or the integrity of the state, will become a reality. Properly evoked, this authority gives the President all he needs to keep the country together and ensure justice for all. Like a true referee, he remains neutral and therefore apparently impotent as long as the game goes on smoothly in accordance with prescribed rules. It is only when there is foul play or the need for redress that his intervention is called for. Only then are his powers revealed. The course of the struggle in the civil war is perhaps our best illustration of the latent but very potent force behind a constitutional authority. Internally it proved that if a cause is truly national, the head of state can always count on the support of the majority of his countrymen even in very trying circumstances. Externally as well, the President can draw on a considerable reserve of authority.

It was not the isolated effort of the rest of Nigeria that defeated the Ibos. Militarily it was a Russian-built air force and British weapons. Politically it was the support of the O.A.U. and the United Nations. The President alone has the right to seek foreign assistance when the security of the country is threatened from an internal or an external source. The possession of this power by the Head of the federal government and the lack of it by the Biafran leader was a decisive factor in the civil war.

An interesting observation regarding armed upheavals in Africa is that practically all the major troubles we have had in our continent—in the Congo, in the Sudan or in Nigeria—are internal clashes involving sections of one national army. There are no examples worth the name of interstate wars between independent African countries. Faced with this situation, the question that arises is whether we lose or gain by making a realistic adjustment, even in the military field, in order to reduce friction between our various communities, or must we remain conventional for convention's sake?

DISPOSITION OF COMMAND IN THE ARMY ON THE EVE OF THE COUP D'ETAT OF JANUARY 1966

COMMANDING OFFICER:
    Major General: Ironsi, East.

BRIGADIERS:
    Military Adviser, London: Ogundipe, West.
    1st Brigade (Kaduna): Ademulegun, West.
    2nd Brigade (Lagos): Maimalari, North.

BATTALIONS:
    1st Battalion (Enugu): Lt. Col. Fajuyi, West.
    2nd Battalion (Ikeja): Lt. Col. Njoku, East.
    3rd Battalion (Kaduna): Lt. Col. Pam, North.
        Lt. Col. Kurubo, East.
    4th Battalion (Ibadan): Lt. Col. Largema, North.
    5th Battalion (Kano): Lt. Col. Ojukwu, East.

HEADQUARTERS:
> G Branch: Lt. Col. Ejoor, Midwest.
>> Major Anwuna, East.
>
> A Branch: Lt. Col. Gowon, North.
> Q Branch: Lt. Col. Unegbe, East.

SPECIAL BRANCHES:
> Engineers: Lt. Col. Banjo, West.
> Ordnance: Lt. Col. Effiong, East.
> Medical: Col. Peters, West.
> Training: Col. Sodeinde, West.
> Academy: Lt. Col. Mohamed, North.
> Reconnaissance: Major Katsina, North.

Chapter 8

TOWARDS A NEW POLITICAL SYSTEM

> With malice towards none; with
> charity for all; with firmness in the
> right, as God gives us to see the
> right, let us strive on to finish the
> work we are in; to bind up the na-
> tion's wounds; to care for him who
> shall have borne the battle, and for
> his widow, and his orphan—to do
> all which may achieve and cherish
> a just, and a lasting peace, among
> ourselves, and with all nations.
>
> Abraham Lincoln
> The Second Inaugural Address
> 4th March 1865.

Need for Positive Leadership

The failure of Nigeria so far as a political experiment can be easily
traced to two main sources:

1. The fact that the politicians played too much politics, often
ignoring national interests in their quest for power or personal
and regional aggrandizement.

2. That even in this game the imbalance in the size of the regions which made up the old Federation precluded the possibility
of taking turns at the control of power at the centre.

The first evil frustrated the enlightened public and nationalists
as a whole; the second frustrated the progressives among the
politicians themselves, were they from the South, like Chief

Obafemi Awolowo or Dr. Michael Okpara, from the Middle Belt, like Mr. Joseph Tarka, or from the Far North, like Aminu Kano.

Most informed Nigerians therefore, except those representing entrenched privilege, had reason to desire a change of the constitution. But on balance our failure has been more the failure of our leadership and our governments rather than that of our peoples—who have not yet found time to discover themselves, or the constitution itself whose success depends largely on the spirit with which it is operated. If a constitution is found to be faulty, given the necessary goodwill and honesty of purpose it can be suitably amended. It is therefore to our leadership that we should direct the appropriate remedial attention.

Unlike Europe for example, where educational and technological advance more or less evolved from basically native institutions, Africa, especially black Africa, is undergoing a revolution. Her peoples are waking up suddenly to new ideas which while bringing new opportunities at the same time introduce new responsibilities. This somewhat brusque introduction of European mechanization and modern life has suddenly opened new vistas of better and softer living. This in turn has developed in the people an enormous but hurriedly-acquired appetite for the good things of life as offered by advanced technology. Where the means are limited the burden placed on the leaders to satisfy this appetite becomes all the greater.

In Nigeria we are lucky to be blessed with very considerable human and material resources. Our major problem has been and still is that of proper political leadership.

In fairness to the few serious and dedicated leaders that we have had, I would like to point out here that while criticizing our past leadership, I do not mean to minimize the difficulties that faced them—difficulties which were legion. Most of these arose from the prevailing ignorance among the masses, a situation which made it not only tempting but easy for unscrupulous political opportunists to thwart the genuine efforts made by the few well-meaning leaders to tackle our problems squarely. The point I am making is that on balance, given both the totality of its liabilities on the one hand and its assets on the other, our collective leadership has made a very poor political investment.

While leadership fared reasonably well at the regional level, especially economically, at the national level too much politicking took place. There was practically no effort made to foster the spirit of nationhood. What, for example, prevented the elected and active head of the Federal Government—the Prime Minister —from visiting each province of the Federation as a matter of national duty at least once a year to make direct contact with the people who, quite independent of the regional setup, directly elected the Federal Parliament over which his government presided?

What serious evidence have we of positive measures undertaken in order to bring home psychologically to the people the important fact, indispensable to the foundation of a nation, that beyond the immediate and limited regional horizon which they see, there lies the fact of a larger nation of which they and their children are part and parcel and to whose fortunes they are irrevocably committed.

Our duty now, if we are to survive, is to create the right conditions for the growth of the right type of leadership capable of wiser investments and better management of our national assets.

In the past the generality of our leaders fell within two major categories: a) those who matched great courage with great ignorance and b) those who though enlightened were lacking in courage in the required measure. Only a tiny few escaped these classifications.

But what we need is not just a handful of capable and dedicated men. To cope effectively with the management of our great endowments in size and potential strength, we need not a few but an entire breed of men and women who combine enlightenment with courage and vigour.

I do not think that ever before in our history have we needed such men and women so badly as now.

Necessary Immediate Steps

Desirable and urgent as it is, the emergence of the required type of political leadership and therefore an assured and stable future for all our people is neither likely to take place overnight nor is it at all possible without durable peace. There can be no better way of advancing its course than putting an immediate end to a fruitless and senseless war. To achieve our purpose, certain clear, direct and practical, though perhaps unsavory, measures appear to me to be totally unavoidable.

1. Restoration of the ante-war constitutional status quo by the suppression of the twelve-state decree, and simultaneous renunciation of the secession which that decree precipitated.

2. Immediate cease-fire with a mixed force of O.A.U. and Commonwealth contingents to supervise it and effectively separate the two armies. The United Nations should send an observer team. The cease-fire terms should include a ban on the importation of arms into the country until certain fixed and agreed conditions are fulfilled.

3. Constitution of a high-powered national relief and rehabilitation committee to work out an extensive programme for repairing war damage throughout the country and for the assessment and payment of compensation to those who merit compensation, from the beginning of the present crisis in January 1966.

4. To help turn the people's mind from war to peace and speed up the relaxation of military tension, a target date for return to civilian rule should be fixed. Determination of such a date to take into consideration the time required for the accomplishment of the following programme before the army withdraws.

a) An accurate census of our population to be carried out exclusively by United Nations' experts and directly supervised by the army.

b) Registration of all Nigerians involving the establishment of birth and death registers in every ward in our cities and every village in the country. This step should be followed by the issue of identity cards to all citizens above fifteen years of age.

As has been stated earlier on, a major defect in our old system is that it left too much room for unscrupulous political careerists to juggle with the very basis of political power in a democratic society—the population at large and the population's voting arm—the electorate. The seeds of distrust sown by the mismanagement of the last population count 1962-1963 demonstrated only too clearly the magnitude of the danger inherent in leaving the determination of such a basic issue in the hands of inevitably partisan political leaders and heads of governments.

Therefore to clear all doubts—and there are many doubts—and start the foundation of our new nation on firm and trusted ground, the problem of our actual population has got to be tackled squarely by a demonstrably impartial body. Any further postponement of this exercise already long overdue will be a major political error. It does not matter whether the existing doubts are founded or unfounded. The important thing is that they do exist and that in order to restore confidence among the people they must be dispelled. The massive shift in population over the last three years and the colossal death toll occasioned by the present war further accentuates the necessity for a fresh count. Once an accurate count is made, the establishment of the system of registration with up-to-date birth and death registers and the issue of identity cards (practised in all French-speaking African countries) should ensure that we do not get involved once more with any population muddle.

c) Reconstitution and transformation of the defunct Ad Hoc Constitutional Conference of September-October 1966 into a well-balanced Constituent Assembly (with expanded membership to include trade unions, students' unions and any other corporate bodies whose contribution could be helpful) to tackle the urgent problem of producing a viable constitution for the country. Draft constitution produced by this body to be subjected to a nation-wide referendum.

d) In the event of mass approval and the adoption of the constitution, organization of elections to both the State Assemblies and the Federal Parliament. The conduct of the elections to be handled exclusively by the army with O.A.U. and Commonwealth observers.

e) Formal handover of government to the newly elected civilian government.

Desirable Changes in the Constitution

A time such as this, in which we find ourselves unhappily engaged in clearing the bloody mess occasioned by errors of the past, is perhaps the most opportune for us to begin to cast our thoughts into the future in search of improvements to strengthen the foundation of the new United States of Nigeria.

The number and seriousness of political disappointments suffered by the nation ever since the attainment of independence, and especially the bitter and costly experience of the past three years, have laid bare important weaknesses not only of our political methods, as mentioned above, but of our political system as well.

These proven weaknesses call for effective reinforcements to a battered and wobbling constitution.

Below are suggestions for amendments.

1. An executive presidency with time limit.
2. Eighteen years voting age limit to admit a higher proportion of our younger and better-informed generation.

3. *a*) Stipulation of conditions for qualification for political parties.

    b) Regulations against parliamentary carpet-crossing to curb the appetite of parliamentary swindlers.

4. Introduction of the "second-ballot" system to ensure fairer parliamentary representation of any particular electoral constituency.

5. A new banner for a new union.

1. Need for Executive Presidency with Time Limit

The question of the headship of state and government is one which should be examined principally from the angle of need—our need as of today. In the old federation, the constitution provided for a largely ceremonial head of state in the person of the president while the prime minister retained full control of the executive power. Like the British model, of which it is a copy, the constitution envisaged the active participation of the opposition in the government—a participation calculated to act as a check on the possible excesses of the prime minister and his parliamentary party.

In the game of actual government, therefore, the president was largely an onlooker who merely kept a record of the scores between the government and opposition. He had no power to interfere directly with the prime minister and could not dissolve Parliament without the advice of the prime minister and his cabinet.

It was therefore clear that the situation facing the nation was one in which the governmental game was carried out without an effective referee. It was precisely on this point that our constitutional practice parted company with its Westminister prototype.

Although today it is clear that the queen, as a constitutional head of state, has no power to interfere in government, British constitutional growth has reached a stage where the intervention of the head of state is not necessary. The concept of government party and opposition party evolved at a time when the government itself was the king's business.

The government party was thus simply that group among the king's subjects helping him with the business of government; the opposition was the group in reserve to be called upon to replace the government group when the king felt the need to change servants. As the idea of subjects in the true feudal sense disappeared and the idea of the people with fixed rights gained strength, the king's relationship with his servants gradually altered. The tragic end of Charles I, the glorious revolution which removed James II from power and the numerous constitutional buffets to which George III was constantly subjected, all these were to alter totally the character and role of the monarchy in Britain. With the growth of the power of his subjects the game of government passed from him to the people and he progressively assumed the role of a referee between the parties.

Today the queen is only a symbolic referee. The effective referee has become an invisible one—a national constitutional conscience imposed by history and maintained by convention.

In Nigeria we had the symbolic referee but not the invisible referee. In practical terms this simply meant that we had no referee at all. In our situation, where the game of politics is both attractive and lucrative and where most of the players are not even familiar with the basic rules, playing without an effective umpire was a clearly irresistible invitation to confusion. Against the background above it can be seen that the old arrangement, which left executive power to the prime minister and his parliamentary group, was unsuitable for our purpose. Once appointed, the prime minister depended solely on his ability to maintain his parliamentary majority to keep power for five years, since only a vote of no confidence passed in Parliament could remove him from office. To keep his power he was thus at the mercy of the parliamentarians. In the case where his own party had a clear and comfortable majority in Parliament he depended on his own parliamentary party alone. He could thus afford to ignore the opposition. And yet this same opposition was intended to be the check on him.

In Nigeria, as in much of Africa today, politicians are a mixed lot and so are the parliamentarians which they produce. Because of the prevailing ignorance and poverty it is relatively easy to buy support among them. A corrupt prime minister can thus get his way irrespective of what the people at large think of his policies and actions.

On the other hand a prime minister who has the knowledge and the will to carry out sound policies finds himself handicapped by the need to keep a constant eye on his parliamentary barometer. To retain enough support he is obliged to bend over and tolerate weaknesses in his parliamentary colleagues without whose backing he cannot keep his power. Such a situation, which encourages corruption and weakness in government, is undesirable. What we need is an arrangement which on the one hand gives enough powers to the head of government to carry out urgent national business but on the other provides an effective, not a theoretical, check on his excesses and possible abuse of power.

The idea of sharing power equally between the president and the prime minister is unworkable in practice. In the first place, unless both of them have totally identical views on everything— an impossible situation—to get things done one of them is bound by sheer superior ability to dominate the other. The Brezhnev-Kosygin duet, certain critics feel, is a heavily strained experiment. For example, the crucial Soviet decision to invade Dubcek's Czechoslovakia (1968) is understood to have had the blessing of Brezhnev only. In Africa, as in many developing countries where we are visibly in a hurry to catch up with the advanced countries, it is not desirable to install in the constitution so many checks and balances that we will in effect produce recurrent governmental stalemates—a situation where those in power can so effectively checkmate one another that nothing moves.

What is required is a head of government who while he is in office is armed with sufficient constitutional power to enable him to carry out effectively the work of governing and, if need be, to force through salutary even if temporarily unpopular measures, but who like the American president is limited in the length of time he can hold that office and wield such extensive powers.

We should think of an executive president popularly elected on a nationwide suffrage for a period of five years and, if the outgoing incumbent is reelected, for a second term of only three years. No one person should be eligible to hold that office for more than eight consecutive years or two broken periods of five years each throughout his entire life. Eight to ten years are enough for any one man to give his best to his nation and people from such a high and demanding position. After that the best in him would have been drained and the dregs if allowed to come out might pollute his good work.

An executive presidency with time limit is a triple guarantee. In the first place the president himself, aware of the fact that he has to quit office compulsorily after a given time, makes efforts to give of his very best and to impress his people while he has the time to do so. This means for him greater efficiency and greater achievement. Secondly, because more often than not his replacement in office would be an opponent, the president takes greater care to avoid any acts that would not bear investigation when he would no longer be in control and when any excesses or indiscretions on his part would be exposed to merciless scrutiny. Thirdly, for the people in general and his opponents in particular, the limit placed on the president's term of office serves as an antidote against his provocations. Consoled by the fact that he has a time limit the president's opponents, thus effectively armed with a constitutional "stopwatch," can better afford to wait for his time to run out rather than run the risks involved in unconstitutional attempts to remove him. This means greater political stability.

The fact that since independence came to African countries no head of state or head of government has quit power without having to be kicked out gives much food for thought. Exceptional ones like our respected President William Tubman of Liberia can pull through for a quarter of a century, but there are not many who are so ordained. In six years, that is between the overthrow of Togo's President Olympio in January 1963 and the recent fall of Mali's Modibo Keita, December 1968, Africa south of the Sahara has seen no less than seventeen coups d'etat. The fact that such distinct and disparate personalities as former President Nkrumah of Ghana and Sir Abubakar Tafawa Balewa of Nigeria both lost power (and one his life) after a decade as head of their respective governments, in the same manner, is in itself an interesting revelation. Despite the vast gulf that separated them they shared a common crime—staying too long in office. Our new constitution should make provision for a compulsory but honourable exit for the holder of the country's highest office.

As far as the method of selection is concerned, it will be necessary that the president be elected directly by the nation at large. This method will ensure that no unqualified person gets to a position of such vital importance through the back door. Nigeria's late Prime Minister Sir Abubakar earned the endearing nickname of Balewa the Good on the merits of his simple virtues among which was his great personal kindness.

Few people who had the privilege of knowing him closely will dispute the fact that all told he was a good and considerate man. But as Nigeria's number one executive he was saddled with a responsibility for which he had the desire but not the training to carry out properly. He was selected by a relatively tiny electorate of simple village farmers who knew nothing about the volume and complexity of government at the national level.

A prospective candidate for the highest national office should be selected by the nation as a whole and on a platform where his ability to fulfill his complex responsibilities in national and international affairs can be properly judged. There are other advantages. The very fact that all the various communities in the country are called upon to unite in the election of one man is in itself an exercise which pushes them further along the path of greater political cooperation, that is, toward greater political unity. A candidate presenting himself to the nation at large, clearly aware of the need to strike a national image, avoids pandering to tribal and sectional interests and makes both his programme and the conduct of his campaign a totally national affair. Once elected, not only are the president's confidence and position reinforced by the reassuring knowledge that he is the choice of the entire nation, he becomes obliged by that very fact to behave nationally.

2. Eighteen Years Voting Age Limit to Admit a Higher Proportion of our Younger and Better-Informed Generation

The justification for limiting voting to only a section of the population in any constitutional arrangement is based on the principle that those who vote and, therefore, decide the fate of the nation should be those in a position of sufficient knowledge and information with regard to the issues upon which they are called upon to vote. This is why, for example, mad people even when they are adults, are excluded from voting. The same reason governed the prescription of a minimum age limit to exclude children.

In ancient times, in most parts of the world, a young man qualified for adulthood when he was judged strong enough to bear arms in time of war or mature enough—that is knowledge-able enough—to participate constructively in the life of his community in time of peace. The choice of the current popular age limit of twenty-one years derives from this same principle. That choice is based only on an estimate of the age at which the average young man (and woman) in a modern society has had about enough time and opportunity to inform himself enough to enable him to participate usefully in the multifarious responsibilities of the society in which he lives. As far as the more technologically advanced countries of today are concerned, this estimate may be fair and reasonable. All that is really involved here is the mere exclusion from universal suffrage in favour of the older, more mature and better-informed citizens, of younger men and women still growing up in the relatively closed world of college and university. In these countries most men and women over the past several decades have had the beneficial influence of literacy and formal education, thus acquiring the mental development that comes with it. In addition there is the advantage that the political systems in which they are operating either evolved *sur place* largely from their native institutions, or were introduced so long a time ago that the people have come to regard them as more or less native. Yet, even in these countries the last decade was marked by a growing demand for a lower age limit.

In much of Africa today the situation is distinctly different. As of now, a high proportion of men and women find themselves strangers to the complex political and administrative machinery transplanted overnight from Europe to Africa by colonial masters and imposed upon a people ill-prepared for the sudden change.

The unhappy result is that a large proportion of our men and women (who are illiterate) while qualifying in every other respect to participate constructively in the community's life and responsibilities suffer, nevertheless, an important handicap when it comes to understanding the complex political machinery of a modern state. Unable to read or write and, therefore, unable to make any direct personal assessment of facts and arguments presented for its judgment and decision, the bulk of the voting population falls easy prey to distorted propaganda and various other forms of political trickery.

Alongside the above situation is the often inadequately appreciated fact that because of the incidence of education, a high proportion of our younger generation—young men and women aged between eighteen and twenty-one years—are considerably more knowledgeable in matters involving national and international politics and especially the latter, than much older adults who can neither read nor write. With such a situation on our hands, it stands to reason that we should reexamine the relevant aspect of the institution bequeathed to us by European colonizers and make the necessary adjustments to admit an important new layer to reinforce the voting structure of our society.

A lower age limit of eighteen years should be introduced as a replacement for the current twenty-one-year barrier.

An additional argument in favour of the above suggestion is that already, in fact although not in theory, a good number of people who have voted during past elections in many parts of the country were actually under the statutory age limit of twenty-one years.

These people fall within two categories: a) young married women under twenty-one upon whom the privileges and responsibilities of adulthood are automatically conferred by the act of marriage itself, and b) the second group is composed for the most part of uneducated young men in the villages, where in the absence of any accurate means of determining age, the problem of qualification for voting was settled by giving the vote to anyone who had begun to earn his own living and who paid tax. Most of these young men, unaffected by the delay which their counterparts suffer while going through the regular gradations of formal education in secondary schools and universities, begin to work for their living at an age sometimes as early as sixteen years.

In this particular case, therefore, we are faced with an anomalous and self-defeating electoral regulation by which uneducated and comparatively uninformed young men under twenty-one years of age are accorded the right to vote—the right to influence and conceivably decide the destiny of the nation—while other young men of the same age whose only disqualification is that they are still engaged in useful studies are legally denied that right.

3. Stipulation of Conditions for Qualification for Political Parties —Regulations Against Parliamentary Carpet-Crossing

Political parties to be recognized and registered for operation in any part of the republic must be national in name and in fact. The exact stipulations for qualification should be carefully studied and clearly set down. The experience of the first republic has shown the dangers inherent in allowing the growth of parties founded on essentially regional interests. Such parties by participating in and, in some cases, by dominating national politics, were attempting to play a role diametrically opposed to that for which they were cast. With rival interests often in serious conflict, a regionally motivated political party which has control of power at the centre, finds itself, for reasons of sheer practical politics, at best vacillating between the interests of the nation on the one hand and those of the particular region from which it draws its strength on the other. At worst it devotes all its energy and attention to exploiting national resources and employing the central governmental apparatus to promote parochial interests.

Alongside the subject of qualification for political parties should be treated the question of parliamentary *carpet-crossing*.

The history of Nigerian parliamentary politics has shown that carpet-crossing has been largely, if not exclusively, in one direction—from the hard opposition bench to soft and lucrative government seats. Greedy and unscrupulous parliamentary pedlars have found it both easy and profitable to sell their seats to a government party in need. Two shattering examples of the extent to which carpet-crossing and unscrupulous shifting of parliamentary alliances were carried out in the past will suffice here.

The first was the 1956 A.G.-N.C.N.C. episode. In the regional election of that year to the Western House of Assembly the scores of both parties at the declaration of results stood as follows:

> N.C.N.C. .... 43 seats
> A.G. .... 37 seats

Then overnight, twenty candidates elected on the N.C.N.C. platform switched their support to Chief Awolowo's A.G. with immediate rewarding results.

The second was in 1962, again in the Western House of Assembly when Chief Samuel Akintola, then premier of the Western Region and deputy leader of the A.G., broke with the A.G. which put him in power, and diverted that party's parliamentary assets into his new party—U.P.P. (United Peoples' Party). This new party without testing its popularity with the Western electorate was able to acquire enough parliamentary support to constitute the government of the Western Region! Similar but smaller episodes occurred frequently in other parts of the country.

To use the money and machinery of a party to secure a seat and then to sell that seat at a profit to that party's opponent is as much an act of political immorality as it is a business swindle. To prevent any such tendency in the future, the constitution should provide effective safeguards.

A man should be free at any time to change his political

alliance when he considers it necessary to do so, but his freedom in this respect should not be such as to encourage acts of political immorality.

Any parliamentarian elected on the ticket of a particular party who later discovers that he disapproves of that party's policies has the right to quit that party but not to impound its assets. He should resign his seat at the same time as his membership of his party and seek a fresh mandate from his constituency to follow his new policy.

4. Introduction of the Second Ballot System

To ensure a fairer and more effective representation of the electorate in any particular constituency, an alteration is necessary in the actual method of determining the success of an election candidate. In the past we have had numerous examples of successful candidates winning their seats with as little as twenty percent of the votes cast by the electorate of their respective constituencies. Such a situation, in effect, means that the candidate declared elected is the choice of only one-fifth of those he represents in Parliament. He therefore represents a minority and not the majority of his constituents—the majority having in effect positively rejected him.

To correct this anomaly, certain countries, France, for example, have adopted the *second-ballot system*. This method stipulates that for an election candidate to be deemed to have won his seat he should score over fifty percent of the actual votes cast in his constituency.

Operating this system in effect means that where there are more than two candidates contesting a particular seat and where no one of them scores over fifty percent of the actual votes cast, a second ballot—a form of elimination contest—will then take place between the first two candidates with the highest scores.

In such a straight fight a simple majority determines the winner. This system therefore makes certain that the representative of any particular constituency is the choice of the majority of the electorate he represents in Parliament.

5. A New Banner for a New Union

After three years of conflict and nearly two of bloodshed unprecedented in our country's history, already with an estimated loss to both sides of some two million souls—most of them Biafran innocents—it is only proper, as one way of honouring the memory of those who have given their lives in this tragic struggle that the emblem of the new Republic born of this conflict should record clearly for all to see the emergence of a new and indissoluble union.

I can conceive of no better form of establishing this record than the fusion, in the flag of our new nation, of the banners under which our heroes on both sides fought and died. Not only would this symbol serve as a constant reminder to generations to come of the result and lesson of an unhappy conflict, but to those on either side who went through the war and survived it, it should bring a measure of consolation that their struggle has not been in vain.

It is for this reason that I recommend a new national flag in which the "green-white-green" receives in its bosom to keep in perpetuity the "rising sun"—the most striking emblem on the Biafran banner.

Epilogues

THE GENESIS OF FAILURE

It is a sad but instructive irony that Lt. Col. Odumegwu Ojukwu, one of Africa's one-time most brilliant political promises, was the man that led his own people with such a lack of ingenuity into what was clearly a foreseeable disaster. This agonizing paradox is resolved only by an understanding of the man.

There are scholars who hold the view that the personality of Adolf Hitler was the factor which more than any other determined the destiny of Second World War Germany, as much indeed, as they argue that Winston Churchill's determined that of Great Britain. Leaning a little on the basic hypothesis of this school of thought, it can be said for the Nigerian civil war that the personality of Odumegwu Ojukwu more than any other single factor determined much of the course and certainly the character of the end of the Biafran adventure. Avid for power, he paid more attention to the politics of the war than to the one basic question of security. Biafra's efforts were trimmed to his size and through much of the conflict reflected his own strength as well as his own weaknesses. This personification of the struggle and the lethal cloud of illusion which it created around him were to persist until the end. Thus on the same day as his more down-to-earth successor, General Effiong, signed the formal act of Biafra's surrender, General Ojukwu was still declaring: "While I live, Biafra lives. If I am no more, it would be only a matter of time for the noble concept to be swept into oblivion."

Ojukwu's political genius was therefore at once his making and his undoing. Because he was an extremely able politican and knew this fact too well, he tended to trust only his own judgment. This fact coupled with an exaggerated personal ambition blinded him to the sickening realities of Biafra's last days. In Biafra two wars were fought simultaneously. The first was for the survival of the Ibos as a race. The second was for the survival of Ojukwu's leadership. Ojukwu's error, which proved fatal for millions of Ibos, was that he put the latter first. A good deal of the war effort was diverted into promoting Ojukwu and his leadership. Be it the question of starvation and relief or other vital matters affecting the population at large, propaganda considerations took precedence over cold realities. Calculation as a method was replaced by hopeful interpretations of ambitious wishes. Personal ambition thus adroitly grafted onto the genuine grievances of an injured people produced a mixture which lacked the purity and sanity that the Ibos needed badly in so unequal a fight. The result was that in the end Biafra secured an undisputed head but not the body of their state.

Right from the start the problem that faced the Ibos in Nigeria was one of security. Sovereignty was only a means to attain this end. As the struggle progressed, it became evident that the chosen means was obstructing progress towards the desired end—*security*. When this fact became clear, many friends inside and outside Biafra began to urge a compromise solution that would recognize Nigeria's territorial integrity but at the same time grant to the Biafrans adequate local autonomy and security. The failure of Biafra's leadership to acknowledge the absolute necessity for a compromise, even in the face of overwhelming odds, not only prolonged the war but ensured that it ended the way it did.

At the beginning of the struggle, the Ibos had a very good chance if not of winning against the authorities in Lagos, certainly of avoiding a humiliating defeat. Politically Ojukwu inherited considerable assets. The political alignment in Nigeria just before the introduction of military rule was by no means unfavourable. Up until the eve of the civil war, Nigerian politics were dominated by the three big tribes: the Hausa-Fulani of the North, the Ibos of the East and the Yorubas of the West. In this triangular fight the key to victory was the combination of any two sides. It did not matter which two. Only the then Northern Region led by the N.P.C. (Northern Peoples' Congress) appeared to have fully appreciated and exploited this golden rule.

After the inconclusive results of the 1959 eve-of-independence federal elections, the N.P.C. brilliantly outmaneuvered its two Southern rivals, the N.C.N.C. (National Council for Nigerian Citizens) then led by Dr. Nnamdi Azikiwe, and the A.G. (Action Group) under the leadership of Chief Obafemi Awolowo. Thwarting a coalition of the two Southern progressive parties, the N.P.C. tinkered out an incongruous alliance with the N.C.N.C. in a lopsided federal coalition government. This move allowed it to rule the country riding on the back of a docile N.C.N.C. When, two years later, the strain of the burden began to tell on the latter, the sensitive rider sought to change horses. The only alternative was the A.G. But strong-willed Awolowo was an obstacle. An attempt to circumvent his rigid political hostility to the N.P.C. led to the vigorous wooing of his deputy, Chief S. L. Akintola, and in turn to the split in the A.G. Backed by the N.P.C.-controlled Federal Government, Akintola succeeded in installing himself and his faction in power in Western Nigeria. Soon, Chief Awolowo and his ablest aides, including Chief Anthony Enahoro, were politically liquidated—incarcerated allegedly for treason. But as events were soon to prove, the people of the West did not want Chief Akintola. Thus, despite an impressive sleight of hand, the N.P.C. succeeded in pulling with it the headship but not the populace of Western Nigeria.

The less sensitive N.C.N.C., dominated by undisciplined, individualistic and greedy federal ministers, woke up too late to appreciate the full political import of the battle for Western Nigeria. Nevertheless the struggle itself revealed to it the risk of isolation involved in its passivity. It set to work for an East-West alliance to fight the federal elections scheduled for 1964. The result was the U.P.G.A. (United Progressive Grand Alliance), uniting the two powerful Southern parties—the N.C.N.C., now led by the dynamic Dr. Michael Okpara, and Chief Awolowo's Action Group led, in his absence, by Alhaji Dauda Adegbenro. U.P.G.A. represented by far the bulk of the population in Eastern, Western, and Mid-Western Nigeria, as well as articulate minority elements in the North, all of whom found common cause in opposing the domination of the conservative and feudal N.P.C.

The military coup of January 1966 swept civilians out of power and dissolved political parties but the undercurrent of East-West solidarity represented by U.P.G.A. remained. Chief Obafemi Awolowo was still serving his ten-year prison sentence. The majority of the Yorubas supported him and his Action Group continued to enjoy abundant popularity in Western Nigeria. His friendship with Dr. Michael Okpara, the Ibo leader of the N.C.N.C., continued to sustain the Southern solidarity. When the counter-coup of July 1966, which brought General Gowon to power, occurred the spirit of that solidarity was still high. The coup itself not only killed the Eastern Ibo leader, General Ironsi, but also the popular Yoruba military governor of Western Nigeria, Lt. Col. Adekunle Fajuyi. In this setting, it was clear that the Yorubas of the West were potentially more inclined to ally with the Ibos of the East against the power of the North from which both had suffered so recently.

General Gowon sensed this mood and acted swiftly. Not only did he release Chief Awolowo immediately from prison, he wooed him with the unprecedented flattery of welcoming him with a guard of honour at Ikeja airport. Gowon's clever release of Chief Awolowo had the effect of reducing but not eliminating Yoruba dislike for the North. This fact soon became evident. In March 1967, Chief Awolowo, now free and still the undisputed leader of the Yorubas, made a public statement which reflected very clearly his sympathy for Col. Ojukwu's Eastern Region. In an open letter to the government, he demanded that the two battalions of Northern troops stationed in the West should be withdrawn from that region which, according to him, was being treated by the Northerners as an occupied territory. He went further to threaten that if "the Eastern Region was pushed out of the federation, Western Nigeria would quit the federation as well." Faced with this threat of an alliance between the Yoruba West and the Ibo East, the Northern controlled Federal Military Government became visibly alarmed.

The seeds of Biafra's failure took root from this point. Eastern Nigeria's leadership failed to appreciate what Gowon saw so clearly—the vital necessity of securing the alliance of Chief Awolowo and the Western Region. Was General Ojukwu simply and innocently overconfident? Or, too anxious for his own position, did he feel that an alliance with Chief Awolowo, already a towering national figure, would dwarf his own fledgling personality and jeopardize his chances for supreme leadership? The fact remains that too little or nothing was done to woo Chief Awolowo. When on 7th May 1967 the Yoruba leader came to Enugu at the head of a reconciliation committee, Ojukwu had a handsome opportunity to play his card. He missed. Dr. Michael Okpara, who still enjoyed popular support in Eastern Nigeria and whose friendship with Chief Awolowo had sustained the U.P.G.A. alliance, was not even invited to meet Chief Awolowo. After a hurried reception, Chief Awolowo's delegation left Eastern Nigeria. Ojukwu saw fit to describe the mission as an "ill-conceived child."

General Gowon on the contrary studiously drew Chief Awolowo closer to himself. He offered him the highest civilian post in the Federal Military Government—the vice-presidency of the Federal Executive Council—with the unspoken understanding that Nigeria was his as soon as the war was over and the army withdrew.

By this act the East-West alliance foreshadowed by U.P.G.A. was destroyed and a new North-West axis was born. From this moment on, Ojukwu's Eastern Nigeria was isolated and when war broke out she had to fight it alone. Eastern Nigeria's political choice of secession completed the region's isolation. The struggle was no longer between the so-called Christian East and Moslem North. That decision united all shades of opinion in Nigeria, giving to them a sense of oneness—and to the Northern-dominated Federal Government an invaluable instrument—in the common fight to defend Nigeria's unity.

Within Eastern Nigeria (Biafra), General Ojukwu's tactics led to a quick alienation of many talented Ibos. From the very beginning he set out to establish his authority with a heavy hand. Under his orders Dr. Michael Okpara, the popular former civilian Premier of Eastern Nigeria, was clamped in jail. So were a number of his ministers. The only notable exception was the former Attorney General, Mr. C. C. Mojekwu, Ojukwu's kinsman, whom he retained and made Biafra's Minister of Interior. Inspired insinuations went round accusing Dr. Azikiwe, Nigeria's former President, of mismanaging the affairs of the University of Nsukka of which he was the founder-chancellor. These political figures were to remain out of favour and far from the corridors of power, except for their occasional utility as window dressing, such as posing for photographs with General Ojukwu or flanking him on ceremonial occasions. Their rich political experience was practically unused and they were called in to participate in the Biafran government in any effective way only when the first signs of collapse had appeared. This was late in September 1967, when Biafra experienced its first military reverses, which led rapidly to the fall of Enugu.

Within the army, General Ojukwu adopted the same tactics of eliminating his opponents. I have already related in the chapter on secession the trend of the struggle for power between Ojukwu and the Biafran army leadership. The result of his success was a timid army tamed to unquestioned obedience. Thus, only two days after General Ojukwu's escape from Biafra, his Chief of Staff, regaining his freedom, was able to declare: "We have always believed that our differences with Nigeria should be settled by peaceful negotiations."

On the diplomatic plane, events were not different. General Ojukwu rejected advice time and again on the need for timely compromise. When the war began to drag on and the suffering of the masses increased steadily, a number of prominent Ibos began to advise General Ojukwu to ask for a confederal arrangement, which while it kept Biafra within Nigeria would nevertheless leave her room for adequate local autonomy. The climax came on the 7th of September 1968, just before the O.A.U. summit meeting in Algiers. A number of anxious Ibos, including Dr. Azikiwe, former President of Nigeria, Dr. Michael Okpara, former Premier of Eastern Nigeria (Biafra), Dr. K. O. Dike, former rector of Ibadan University, and myself, made a formal recommendation in which we told General Ojukwu that as Africa was sympathetic to the Ibo cause, but at the same time opposed to secession, he should use the opportunity of the Algiers meeting to seek O.A.U. guarantees for a confederal arrangement such as was agreed at Aburi (Ghana). General Oukwu not only rejected this advice outright but asked some of us to recant or resign. Dr. Azikiwe left Paris in disgust and went to London in voluntary exile. I myself chose to resign.

It is here perhaps that the question of the responsibility of a timid Ibo elite comes in. The Biafran masses, enslaved by an extremely efficient propaganda network and cowed by the iron grip of a ruthless military machine, had neither the facts nor the liberty to form an independent opinion. The case of the elite was different. Biafra's choice was clear after the double losses of (a) territory, with the fall of Biafra's major towns, Enugu, Port-Harcourt, Calabar, Onitsha, Aba and Umuahia and (b) war funds, with the exhaustion of Biafra's treasury in February 1968 caused by Nigeria's switch to a new currency which suddenly rendered practically valueless some thirty million pounds in Biafran hands. Those who had access to the facts knew that the time had come to seek a realistic way to end the war and save millions of defenseless Ibos and innocent children from disaster. In private they expressed this view but proved too cowardly to take a stand and tell Ojukwu the truth. On the contrary, they allowed themselves to be used for the public denunciation of those who took the risk of calling for a halt. Yet, when their cherished handiwork was threatened with collapse, these front-line advocates of "fighting to the last man" were the first men to flee.

One particular episode has since stuck in my mind. In June 1968, I paid my first of two visits that year to Tunis as a member of an official delegation headed by Dr. K. O. Dike and including Mr. Francis Nwokedi to present Biafra's case to the Tunisian government. During our discussion, President Bourguiba twice referred to a loose federal arrangement and at the end of that conversation, asked directly what we thought of such an arrangement. Dr. Dike looked up. Mr. Nwokedi, a one-time Ironsi confidant and General Ojukwu's private eye on the delegation, signalled disapproval. The answer came: "It is too late, Your Excellency, to think of a confederation or anything like that at this stage. That was agreed at Aburi, but Lagos rejected it. After so much sacrifice we are not prepared to go back to it." President Bourguiba sat back in his chair. We missed the cue. Back to Tunis Hilton. I reopened the matter at the dinner table. I suggested that we were wrong to have given so direct an answer rejecting a confederal arrangement. I thought the right step was to have simply made a note of President Bourguiba's question and relayed it with our recommendations to General Ojukwu. Mr. Nwokedi was infuriated. "You mean we should surrender," he asked through a choking mouthful of caviar. Dr. Dike rushed to my defence: "That's not what Raph said; he is merely giving his opinion." I left the table and my meal. I had had enough.

The termination of the conflict in Biafra's unconditional surrender was by no means inevitable. Despite the ultimate advantages that lay with the federal side in military superiority and international support accruing to a widely recognized sovereign state, the struggle hung in the balance long enough to give the Biafran leadership ample room for fruitful diplomatic maneuver. It was its stark refusal to take timely advantage of a prolonged military stalemate that spelt Biafra's doom.

The Commonwealth-sponsored peace talks in Kampala (May 1968) were an important watershed in the development of the Nigerian conflict. Although their failure closed the door for good to Commonwealth initiative, it opened it wider for active African diplomatic intervention. That courageous but abortive attempt awakened the dormant and timid O.A.U. Consultative Peace Committee to the consciousness that after all there were two sides to the conflict, even though both sides formed one Nigeria. It was thus that for the first time serious direct approaches were made to the Biafran leadership and in mid-July 1968, General Ojukwu was invited to address the committee in Niamey, capital of the Niger Republic.

From this moment on, the key to victory lay in the diplomatic rather than in the military field. Neither Nigeria nor Biafra produced its own arms in any serious sense of the term. Both were fed—one lavishly, the other meagerly—through umbilical cords leading from the exterior—from the big powers. Because the interest of these powers in Africa is largely a global one aimed at winning the maximum of influence in the continent, it was evident that none of them could knowingly go seriously against any clear trend of African opinion, especially on such a matter with momentous implications for the entire continent. In spite of the widespread sympathy for the Ibos provoked by the massacres of 1966, Biafra's secession, like its Katangan predecessor, found very limited sympathy among the ruling classes in Africa. The O.A.U. stuck faithfully throughout the struggle to the principle of settlement "within the context of one Nigeria."

Though lacking military might, this organization provided a preponderant moral force which in turn sustained Nigeria's international support. The two big powers—Britain and Russia—who backed Lagos used the smoke screen of massive African approval to promote their own interests. The United States drew solace from it for its neutrality. France, whatever might have been her secret wishes, could not in her own interest advance beyond a certain point to help *le pauvre petit Biafra*. Throughout much of the war, Biafra's lone powerful backer was France. Her active and wholehearted intervention was the only real chance Biafra had to "make it." Yet by 9th September 1968, General de Gaulle had made it abundantly clear that "In this matter France has aided and aids Biafra *within possible limits*. She has not taken steps to accomplish the final decisive act—the recognition of the Biafran Republic—because she considers that the matter is *above all the affair of Africans*."[1] [author's italics]

In such an assisted tournament the determining factor was the relative strength of the seconds. General Ojukwu saw the opponent in front but ignored his powerful backer. Realistic planning based on timely concessions was replaced by virulent but ineffectual invective against "neo-colonialist Britain" and "revisionist Russian imperialism." Yet all that was needed to avoid disaster was a timely placation of the humbler and more accessible African opinion—African fears about secession—by abandoning the demand for sovereignty for the *substance of security* in a loose Nigerian union.

The guarantee of support for such a moderate stand existed. While few African heads of states were prepared to go as far as Tanzania, Ivory Coast, Zambia and Gabon in giving full international recognition to Biafra, there were nonetheless many who were not enthusiastic supporters of the rigid and sometimes arrogant federal line. What mattered most to the bulk of African opinion was that the principle of secession should be dropped. The leaders in Senegal, Tunisia, Sierra Leone, Uganda, Liberia, Burundi, Rwanda and Dr. Busia's Ghana were clearly among those in this middle position. By refusing to take the initiative to abandon secession, Biafra refused to help these potential allies within the O.A.U. to come more effectively to her aid.

Thus did an insensitive group clinging to sovereignty at all costs succeed in taxing to exhaustion the resources of one of Africa's most gifted races. The cause for which the Ibos fought and died—to ensure their inalienable right to a decent life in adequate security—was and still remains a just one. It was the leadership's inability to distinguish between its own limited interests and those of the Ibos as a race that brought them disaster.

In contrast with the unrealism of Biafran leaders, General Gowon clearly appeared to have grasped the crucial importance of African support as indeed, as I mentioned earlier in this chapter, he had foreseen the vital need for alliances within the country itself. This was in connection with the flattering attention he paid to Chief Awolowo and his tactful attitude which ultimately secured for him the alliance of the "leader of the Yorubas." From the start, he wooed the O.A.U. with the same assiduity. The different attitudes paid off accordingly. At the Algiers Summit Conference in September 1968, President Kaunda, who led his country's delegation, made an impassioned plea for Biafra's cause. Biafra not only received the direct support of the four countries that had recognized her, two countries, Burundi and Rwanda, refused to take sides by abstaining. A year later, at the Addis Ababa Summit (September 1969) President Julius Nyerere came fully prepared to press Biafra's case for sovereignty. He lobbied delegates actively and distributed a prepared statement aimed at convincing his colleagues that they were wrong in supporting the federal government's case. He was categorical:

> The break-up of Nigeria is a terrible thing. But it is less terrible than that cruel war. Thousands of people are being shot, bombed or seeing their homes and livelihood destroyed; millions, including the children of Africa, are starving to death. (It is estimated that possibly more people have died in this war in the last two years than in Vietnam in the last ten years). We are told that nothing can be done about this. It is said that the sufferings of the Biafrans in the war are regrettable, but that starvation is a legitimate war weapon against an enemy. Yet by this statement you have said that these people, the Nigerians and the Biafrans, are enemies, just as Britons and Germans in Hitler's war were enemies. If that is the case, it is rational to imagine that, once a federal victory is obtained, they can immediately be equal members of one society, working without fear? Or is the logic of being enemies not a logic which leads to conquest and domination when one side is victorious? . . . Let us reject the internal domino theory in relation to the Nigerian question. For it assumes that the people now in the Federation of Nigeria are, and wish to be, imperialists. I cannot believe that.
>
> I still believe that they are capable of recognizing the tragedy which has caused one part of the federation to break away, and of acknowledging that very different tactics are necessary if the old Nigeria is ever to be recreated. For surely they could decide to leave the Biafrans to go their own way and, by the kind of Nigeria which they create, to show the Biafrans what they are losing by remaining separated from their brethen. For if the other peoples of Nigeria decide to work together, they will continue to be a strong and powerful force in Africa; they really have the opportunity to build a good nation of which every Nigerian—indeed every African—can be proud. Then it may be that at some time in the future the Biafrans will wish to rejoin the peoples from whom they now wish to part; if this happens, it will be the accession of a free people to a large and free political unit.[2]

In the face of this "provocation," Gowon's response was characteristic. Against the advice of his hawks, who regarded Nyerere's action as a slap in the face, he sought an interview with the Tanzanian president "to explain how reluctant he was to continue the war." He also met the leaders of the three other delegations from the countries that had recognised Biafra. The result of his "humble" initiative was predictable. At the close of the meeting, the case for Biafra's sovereignty did not have a single direct supporter. Of the forty-one countries attending, all but five voted in support of Lagos, for settlement "within the context of one Nigeria." Only Sierra Leone joined Tanzania, Zambia, Gabon and the Ivory Coast in merely abstaining. The echoes of that meeting went beyond the membership of the O.A.U. In early October 1969 when President Nyerere paid an official visit to Canada, the following report underlined the extent of his conversion:

> Tanzania is one of the four states that have recognized Biafran statehood and Canada is very emotionally involved at the moment in this issue. It is believed that President Nyerere feels that the Canadian government should *concentrate on relief efforts to Biafra rather than on overt political action,* although he would no doubt welcome any pressures by Ottawa on Whitehall to stop supplying arms to the Lagos government.[3] [author's italics]

Seeking an explanation for the source of the impulse behind Ojukwu's undoubted personal domination of the Biafran situation, Nelson Ottah, former editor of *Drum* and a high ranking member of the Biafra's elite Directorate of Propaganda during the war, commented as follows:

> Perhaps Emeka, were he born to another father, might not have aimed so high and fallen so low. But being the son of his father and his mother, he had too wide a lee-way to make up. His father was too rich and of high standing in the estimation of the Ibos. Emeka craved for a heroic act that would make him greater than his father. His mother has children to another man, and Emeka himself was born out of wedlock. Emeka craved for an achievement that would force his admirers to forget his birth. What turned Emeka into a bedroom Napoleon was a complex of inadequacy.[4]

The above probably is an oversimplification which tends to debase the issue somewhat by reducing it to a mere craving on Ojukwu's part to overcome a complex resulting from the ordinary accident of birth. It was not his birth; it was his upbringing that exercised the decisive influence on Ojukwu, shaped his early life and conditioned his reactions when he found himself later in power. Frederick Forsyth, a close wartime friend with a strong pro-Biafran bias, records the following about Ojukwu's early life:

> The story of his second, but favourite son, can hardly be described as a rags-to-riches tale. The family dwelling where the young Emeka Ojukwu played before going to school was a luxurious mansion. Like most wealthy businessmen, Sir Louis kept open house and his mansion was a meeting place for all the moneyed elite of the prosperous colony. In 1940 the young Ojukwu entered the Catholic Mission Grammar School, but soon moved to King's College, the smart private academy modelled closely on the lines of one of Britain's public schools. Here he remained until he was thirteen; when his father sent him to Epsom College, set amid the rolling green hills of Surrey. He recalled later that his first impression of Britain was a sense of being completely lost 'amid this sea of white faces.' The isolation of a small African boy in such a totally strange environment caused the first moulding of the character that was to follow. Driven in on himself he developed a private philosophy of total self-reliance, an unyielding internal sufficiency that requires no external support from others.[5]

To this special development of his ego and the feeling of self-sufficiency was added the confidence acquired from an Oxford University *milieu* and from the fact of his father's great wealth. Back to Nigeria Ojukwu soon joined the army, where as an officer he got more accustomed to giving orders and receiving prompt obedience than meeting opposition and arguments. Furthermore, as one of the first and very few indigenous graduate officers of his time, he enjoyed an immense prestige even among his fellow officers. Once again he found himself more often at the 'giving' rather than at the 'receiving' end. Such a combination of circumstances could hardly have failed to leave its mark on his character and bearing. By keeping Ojukwu constantly enveloped in an atmosphere of superiority, it made him, as a matter of habit, distrustful and disdainful of other people's judgment, impatient with their opinions and finally simply authoritarian.

The extent of Ojukwu's anxiety and determination to control the most minute detail of the actions of even his ablest and most "trusted" lieutenants is perhaps well illustrated by the following routine query he sent on 25th July 1968 to Dr. Eni Njoku, former vice-chancellor of the University of Nigeria, Nsukka, who was then leading the Biafran delegation to the preliminary peace talks in Niamey, capital of Niger Republic: "B.B.C. reports this morning a member of the Biafran delegation, apparently the leader, as coming out from the conference hall hugging with a Nigerian. Would like clarification of this report which, if it is true, is a breach of my instructions that there should be no fraternization between us and the enemy."

The above analysis of Biafra's failure has evidently put strong emphasis on the role of Ojukwu's personal leadership. Such an approach, no doubt, raises the following important question: How is it possible for one man—a young and largely inexperienced soldier at that—to impose his will for so long on some fourteen million people among whom is to be found one of the highest concentrations of the intelligent and educated elite of black Africa?

Perhaps the following testimony from Philip Effiong, the forty-four-year old veteran to whom Ojukwu handed power, will throw some light on the answer to this question. In an exclusive interview published in the monthly magazine *Drum* of April 1970, we find the following questions and answers.

Drum:
    One would expect that those army officers who did not approve of secession, would give Ojukwu a showdown. Why did you not remove him by organising a bloodless coup d'etat?

REFLECTIONS ON THE NIGERIAN CIVIL WAR

Effiong:

It wasn't easy. Make no mistake about it. The sentiment of the people was very strong in favour of the ideas and ideals propounded by Emeka. I hate to say this because it makes me feel like a coward. Ojukwu was a dictator, you know. It wasn't always safe or easy to oppose his ways or will. The best you could do was to point out the dangers to Ojukwu. But if you didn't know when to stop shooting your mouth, he could easily throw you in detention.

Drum:

What virtues did you find in Ojukwu?

Effiong:

He was no devil. Everybody admires his personal courage, his infinite ability for hard work (because that man could go on from morning almost indefinitely). He was quite courageous, although in the end he escaped. But he had one weakness—he did not know when to apply the brakes. But it's purely because he was ambitious. He was a very able chap.[6]

Indeed, for anyone close to the scene and who saw the mechanism of power at work in Biafra, the answer to that question holds no mystery. Ojukwu inherited three major assets which worked in his favour and which he exploited to the full to ensure for himself ultimately an almost hysterical support from the Biafran masses. As the son of one of Nigeria's wealthiest men, he belonged to the establishment, whose confidence and respect came naturally to him. As an Oxford-educated young man, he found easy acceptance among the intellectual elite—in the civil service and especially concentrated in the University of Nsukka, which provided most of the intellectual force behind the Biafran revolution. Then finally, the masses of aggrieved Ibos gave him their unconditional support because they saw in him a leader with the necessary toughness and the will to challenge Lagos and avenge them for their bitter experiences and the massacres of 1966 —acts for which they held the old Northern region and the then Northern-controlled Federal Military Government responsible.

This combination of support from the various sections of the population produced a tripod power base impossible to topple as long as the threat to the people's security existed. With the masses blindly but resolutely behind him, even his colleagues in the army who disagreed with Ojukwu were powerless to act against him. The few who tried to oppose him paid dearly and promptly. It is a measure of Ojukwu's political cleverness that he made a most remarkable use of that situation. Perhaps his single but fatal error was that he made a *personal* rather than a *public* use of the unprecedented popular support ever given to a black African leader in comparable circumstances within living memory.

NOTES

1. "Afrique Occidental—Nigéria. De Gaulle et le Biafra," *A.F.P. Bulletin* (Author's transl.).
2. Julius K. Nyerere, *The Nigeria/Biafra Crisis*, 4 September 1969. (This paper was distributed by the Tanzanian delegation to participants at the O.A.U. Summit Conference in Addis Ababa—September 1969).
3. *The Times* (London), 3 October 1969.
4. *Drum* (Lagos, Nigeria), April 1970.
5. Frederick Forsyth, *The Biafran Story* (Harmondsworth, Middlesex, 1969), pp. 63-64.
6. *Drum* (Lagos, Nigeria), April 1970.

AN ELASTIC FEDERAL UNION

The Question of States Reexamined

I would like to reopen the states issue with the following three extracts culled from the maiden issue of *Fume*.[1] Between them they summarize our problems as of today, by bringing out vividly the fact that fear of domination—political and economic —not only prompted the creation of the twelve states but still persists after their creation.

On the origin of the twelve states by Dr. Emiko Afimomo.

> The power struggle in Nigeria has never been a struggle be-tween majority groups stricto senso. It is neither a struggle between the Hausa-Fulani and the Ibos. It is a struggle between the majority and the minority groups who had often clamoured for the creation of more states because they often found them-selves left out in the share of the "National Cake" . . . Such was the position when the head of state, General Yakubu Gowon, called a Constitutional Conference in 1967 to resolve the Nigerian crisis. During this conference, while the majorities were opting for a confederal structure for Nigeria, the minorities, with the Midwest taking the lead, energetically demanded a federal struc-ture for fear of being absorbed by the larger groups. The Mid-west stand fortunately found echo with the minority. Tivs of the North who had always clamoured for a Middle Belt State and the minorities of the Eastern region who had often demanded a Calabar-Ogoja-Rivers State. This was how we have come to have a federal structure of twelve states.

On revenue allocation by Taiwo Idemudia.

In which ever way a federation evolves, the problems of fiscal and financial relations of the centre and the component units and the financial dependence of one or more units on others are always present. In fact, they are the greatest tests of any federation.

As a criterion for revenue allocation, the regions have always laid emphasis on "derivation" if they are economically buoyant and have been protagonists of "national interest and even progress" only when they are comparatively poor. The West, (with her cocoa) in the days of export duties prominence, threw her weight on "derivation" while the East struggled tooth and nail for "even progress and national interest." The positions of the two regions reversed dramatically after the discovery of mineral oil in the East.

We are in a federation, so the states should be given fiscal autonomy and allowed to manage their finance within the limit of their resources . . . Every state at present needs its revenue to carry out much needed development projects. Dr. P. N. C. Okigbo gave an insight into this problem in his book—*Nigerian public finance*—when he warned that any attempt to subsidise and give grants to units of the federation without due consultation with and approval of the so-called well-to-do parts of the country will lead to abuse of power in the centre, interstate animosities and feuds as well as charges of favouritism. *We have to face the facts and be frank; while the American understood why a Kennedy appointed a Kennedy to his cabinet, a Nigerian cannot understand why a Gowon should do the same if he does. We just have not developed up to that stage.*

On the fear of domination by Ojo Igbinoba.

A glance at the map of the new states of Nigeria will convince even the casual observer that some of the new states are too big in terms of size and in terms of population. I want to repeat once more that one of the guiding principles of federalism is that no one or two states shall be able to over-rule and bend the will of the central authority to its own will. For instance, North-Eastern state, comprising Bornu, Adamawa, Sardauna and Bauchi provinces has an area of 103,639 square miles and a population of approximately 7.8 millions. This does not include the area of Sardauna province. The North-Western state comprising Sokoto and Niger provinces, has an area of 65,143 square miles and a population of approximately 6 millions.

Although separated by the small Kano state, *the spectre that is haunting me is whether the North-Eastern state and the North-Western state will not be able to combine to over-rule and bend the will of the central authority to their own advantage. The possibility is not remote.*

Another large state is the Western state with an area of 29,100 square miles and a population of 9.5 millions. Although it has been said that the present structure of states is not permanent, it is the opinion of the writer that as soon as the cessation of the civil war, these three big states should be further carved up, if necessary *by decree.*[1] [author's italics]

In reexamining my earlier recommendations on the issue of states (vid. Chapter V) I find these excerpts of particular interest. The authors, two of whom are students and one a young university lecturer, represent an important class in the new Nigeria. They all come from the Mid-West—a state which has the dual attributes of being not only "Nigeria in miniature," because of its multitribal composition, but has spearheaded the minority emancipation movement in the country.

The first confirms my earlier assertion that the particular choice of twelve states was motivated by an exaggerated, even though very legitimate, desire on the part of Nigeria's minorities to abolish their fear of domination by the bigger tribes.

The second reflects the existing local jealousies and fears of economic domination of the states by the centre.

The third pinpoints the problem of tribal or regional domination but misses the answer to it. Its author stresses, for instance, the likelihood of regroupment by parts of the former Northern region and the possibility of such a combination succeeding in practice in dominating the central government. Yet as an answer to this danger he recommends merely a further splitting of the same large states. He is correct in his assessment that for some time to come divisions made on the map will be clearer on paper than in the minds of many Nigerians. If, as he points out, some of the present states can easily combine to dominate the centre, an interesting question arises. What difference does it then make if the same states are simply split further?

Indeed, the smaller the new units the lesser their chances of influencing the centre independently and therefore the greater the temptation to try to gain weight by regroupment. When this happens, old habits, cultural and ethnic affinity are bound to come into play. Once more, we shall find ourselves saddled with an all-powerful central government manipulated to partisan advantage by one clever section of the country.

Until we become a truly integrated nation—only time, tolerance and patience will make this possible—it is unrealistic to adopt a constitution which presupposes the existence of an already integrated society. What we need in the interval between our present realities and that future ideal is a constitutional "sliding scale" which, operating from a guaranteed national base, allows easy adjustment to the various phases of our growth towards national adulthood. The answer lies in "modulated" decentralization within the framework of a federation in which minority elements are effectively insulated from the threat of domination by any of the preponderant tribes, Hausa-Fulani, Ibo and Yoruba.

It is perhaps appropriate here to recall briefly my treatment of the question of states. I did and still regard the creation of states in Nigeria as essential for stability in the federation. My criticism of the present twelve-state structure had been twofold. The first was that it was imposed by military decree (27th May 1967)—without consultation whatever with the Eastern government—and in consequence precipitated, barely three days afterwards, the secession of that region on 30th May 1967. This led a few weeks later to the outbreak of war. To the above extent therefore, it was a *casus belli*. This was the consideration, while the war was on, behind my recommendation for its abolition as a *quid pro quo* for Biafra's renunciation of secession as a basis for a cease-fire. That cease-fire was achieved otherwise.

The second criticism emanated from my view that the number twelve was perhaps too high, giving rise to a multiplicity of feeble states too weak to bear the responsibilities which increased local autonomy (which I advocated) would of necessity impose on them.

Since writing the earlier part of the book, I have had occasion to discuss these points with fellow Nigerians. Their intelligent criticisms of some of my ideas, especially of my proposal regarding six states, have shed considerable light on my views. While I believe that the basis of my recommendation still retains its force, I have been only too happy to benefit from these criticisms. The ultimate question of the number of states is perhaps best left to a representative Constituent Assembly to thrash out.

Dangers in Overcentralization

Whatever number of states is finally decided upon by the entire Nigerian people, an important point to bear in mind is that recurrent experience has shown that *in our present stage of political development*, a loose rather than a tight arrangement holds out the best chances of peaceful coexistence among our numerous ethnic and cultural elements.

The case for greater local autonomy rests on two pivots; the first is *inter-state relationship*, involving the states as units. The second, relating to individual citizens, is the *movement of people from one state to the other*. One of the major weaknesses of the Balewa federation was that it combined the disadvantages of both tightness and looseness. This hybrid character made it susceptible to contradictory exploitation. The N.P.C. dominated Federal Government, which ruled the country from independence to the coup of January 1966, used the excuse of a strongly centralized army to its own political advantage. The most vivid example of this constitutional manipulation appeared during the struggle for power in the Western Region in the early sixties, between Chief Awolowo, the Action Group leader, and his deputy, Chief Akintola. Although the matter was nominally the affair of the people of the Western Region, it was nevertheless resolved by influences and interests external to the people of the West. In that "democratic" contest it was the strong arm of the N.P.C. dominated Federal Government, not the people of the West, that chose the government of the West. Akintola's minority faction was forcibly planted on the Western electorate. The seed of popular discontent was thus sowed in the West. A bloody uprising followed another attempt at a "repeat performance" during the 1965 West regional elections.

Such examples of past abuses only underline the necessity of avoiding a constitutional arrangement which provides both the temptation and the means to a central government to toy successfully with matters of vital local interest to the people of any given state in the federation. It was indeed the successful interference in the affairs of the Western Region by the central government in the first five years of independence that kept that region in a state of perpetual turmoil, provoking the revulsion and disgust at the national level that led directly to the coup of January 1966.

To be operated with equity the conventional strong centre must presuppose a "free-for-all" atmosphere throughout the country. This means in practical terms unrestricted freedom of movement for our national labour force and preferential treatment for Nigerian citizens vis-à-vis foreigners in matters of employment throughout the country. Yet, in many vital matters affecting the population's daily existence, the same party in power at the centre would choose to invoke the looseness of the federal arrangement. In such cases, the "North for the Northerners," the "West for the Westerners," the "East for the Easterners," etc., became valuable slogans. Thus in order to protect regional interests, expatriate doctors and lawyers were preferred to their

Nigerian counterparts. In the North for example, Northern leaders, anxious to prevent a flooding of Southerners into the North to "usurp" places earmarked for a future Northern generation, imported Pakistani doctors and lawyers en masse.

Between 1962 and 1963, as an official of the Nigerian High Commission in Karachi, I participated at several interviews for the recruitment of doctors. The High Commissioner Alhaji Abdulkadir Koguna, an affable extrovert, had a favourite question which featured regularly on our lists. "What are you—sunni or ahmadiya?" (Moslem religious sects). The former was a qualification, the latter was taboo. Surely, such a qualification, apart from its undoubted merits in getting the soul of the candidate closer to salvation, was hardly a serious criterion for determining his suitability for medical service to Nigeria's needy millions. But those were the facts. Today, the class of leaders that interpreted Nigeria's needs in those terms is largely gone. But these needs remain. Unequal educational development and differences in social habits have yet to be overcome.

On the one hand, it is only fair that people from those parts of the country which are, for the time being, less developed should be protected from being permanently "submerged" by their compatriots who, because of greater educational facilities, are at present better equipped to occupy key professional posts in the country's administration. Practical allowance has got to be made to protect the interests, especially of the future generation, of those Nigerians from the educationally less favoured areas. On the other hand, the opposite extreme should be avoided. It is not easy for a Yoruba, Ibo, or Efik medical doctor to understand why a foreigner will have a better chance of employment in certain parts of Nigeria while at the same time funds accruing from his own area flow freely into those same parts of the country *"in the interest of oneness and national unity."*

An all-powerful central government, controlling the bulk of the national purse and economic development should, in the interest of fairness, involve a monolithic arrangement steam-rolling re-gional, political and economic protectionism. Free movement of development funds aimed at achieving *even* economic develop-ment throughout the country is fair and indeed necessary for future equilibrium and prosperity among all the citizens of Nigeria. But this freedom of movement of funds conceived *in the interest of all* cannot go smoothly and equitably hand in hand with restrictive measures conceived *in the interest of a few.* The less developed sections of the country have every right to expect financial and other forms of assistance from the other parts of the country. Unfortunately, in our present circumstances, even the so-called favoured areas have enormous economic problems of their own far beyond their immediate capacity to solve. The Mid-West and the Rivers States, for example, which today pro-duce the bulk of Nigeria's foremost cash-earning commodity—oil —have enough pressing needs of their own to absorb the totality of the revenue accruing to Nigeria from the production of oil. Sharing this income with the rest of Nigeria is, of course, a healthy sacrifice in the interest of national unity. They are likely to continue to accept this fact willingly as long as there is no cause for them to feel that the sacrifice is one-sided.

Our political and tribal conflicts are merely symptoms, not causes, of a basic economic plague. As in most developing coun-tries, far too many people are struggling for a share of too small a national cake. To get the better of other competitors in this contest, our leaders fall easy prey to the temptation of employing the most effective weapon in African society today—tribal and cultural differences. In this struggle it is thus the national desire to win that actually evokes and abuses differences due to varying ethnic origins, differences which in themselves are a harmless and natural anthropological phenomenon. In fact, as a rich source of cultural variety, these differences constitute a positive asset for any community. Properly harnessed, there is everything to gain from our variegated cultural heritage.

However, because in their very variety they define easily recognizable social and cultural frontiers, these differences are susceptible to abuse if employed to encourage division among the people. It is the existence of acute economic needs and therefore of a fierce politico-economic struggle that confers exaggerated importance to differences in ethnic origins. Thus while, for example, within Nigeria we have had bloody explosions and a state of quasi-permanent tension between Ibos and Yorubas, or Hausas and Ibos, or Yorubas and Hausas, the same tribal differences have never opposed the Ibos of Nigeria with the Yorubas of Dahomey or with the Hausas of the Niger Republic. The simple explanation is that despite the same differences in ethnic origins, the Ibos are not engaged in a contest for any national cake with the Yorubas or Hausas outside Nigeria.

It is clear that in the charged atmosphere such as we have, and will continue to have for some time, the process of detonating tribal and sectional tension and therefore, of reducing the chances of sectional conflict in Nigeria, is directly linked with reducing to the safest minimum the areas of potentially dangerous conflict between opposing cultural tendencies within the Nigerian federation. This means greater decentralization. Our *transitional* constitutional arrangement should be aimed at doing just that, while we concentrate our efforts in the immediate future on positively employing our educational system to giving the new generation of Nigerians an appropriate national orientation. This is how the baneful side of tribalism will die a true and natural death. Ethnic and cultural differences are not easily effaceable. The Walloons and Flemings in Belgium are still struggling with theirs. The Swiss made a realistic accommodation for their own.

While these problems are not of such a character that the only answer to them is total separation, their very existence counsels a cautious and realistic approach to union. General Gowon thought and said so only four years ago:

In my earliest statement to the nation after assuming office, I made it quite clear then that the basis of a restoration of peace and confidence was by returning to the status quo as events had proved that *an over-centralized administration cannot be maintained in a country like ours.*[2]

The building of a stable and powerful Nigerian nation, like all gigantic constructions, requires time. Although the ultimate objective has of necessity to be a solidly integrated nation, advance towards this noble objective could be marred by inadequate attention to the realities that yet divide our peoples. The combination of increased local autonomy for the states and the institution of a nationally-elected executive presidency (as I will attempt to show later) holds out the highest hope for a peaceful advance towards this goal.

A conventional strong central government could, of course, be imposed immediately by military might, but this method involves a double risk. The first is that it can only be achieved at the expense of a section of the country by the imposition of the will and taste of those who now control the levers of power on the remainder of their compatriots. Simply because such a situation is unlikely to be tolerated indefinitely, eventual attempts to reverse it will mean political instability. The second is that for a composite nation like ours, involving the army too deeply for too long in purely political activities is likely to subject it to severe political strains, which in turn could affect its discipline and unity. This was, in fact, to some extent what happened in 1966 when the Nigerian army involved itself in politics. Exposed to political influences, the proud tradition of the Nigerian army, regarded unitl then as the model of national integration, gave way before the bitter realities of sectional politics.

After the coup of January 1966 and the disappearance of the much discredited old regime, the only evident feeling in the country was that a new era was born, that sectionalism was gone.

Reflecting the prevailing ambiance of optimism, an editorial in Nigeria's foremost independent newspaper, the *Daily Times*, saw the future in these terms:

> Something just had to be done to save the federation. Something has been done. It is like a surgical operation which must be performed, or the patient dies. The operation has been performed. It has proved successful, it is welcome. We have trust in the head of the new federal military government. We are satisfied that he is capable of bringing peace that has eluded us for so long; we believe that he is capable of restoring law and order in this strife-torn country of ours. He can redeem the fortune of the federation and put it on the high road of unity, tranquility and success.[3]

Yet the truth of the matter was that only those who profited from the coup saw this hope. Those who lost by it were mute. They did not agree with the new order but they were in no position to make their disagreement known. This false calm and false hope were soon to vanish when the defeated elements regained their voices and their freedom of action. The July countercoup was the result.

Nigeria's unity and greatness can only be truly achieved by the genuine dedication of those who have more love for Nigeria and her people than the desire to use both to promote the interests of any given group. Such a task requires the capacity to strike a genuine equilibrium between the desire to build a powerful and prosperous modern state and genuine concern for the liberty of the multifarious cultural elements and groups that make up the country. Walking together in the right spirit with few but important links will allow us time to learn how to move together while respecting our differences.

If there is anything which the last four years has taught us it should be the need for patient spadework. It is hardly considered a waste of time or a backward step to start work on a skyscraper aimed towards the heavens by first of all digging patiently deep in the opposite direction—downwards. The duty of our generation is to lay a solid and stable foundation. From this sure base will rise the type of structure, the *image*, but not yet the *reality* of which we have before us now.

An Elastic Machinery

In considering the division of responsibilities between the centre and the states, the point of cardinal importance is not so much one of merely allotting spheres as it is that of how these responsibilities are carried out in practice.

Thus our objective should be not simply that of giving more or fewer responsibilities than before to the states vis-à-vis the centre but of producing a new basis for a joint venture, with the states having more practical opportunities to operate *sans friction* in many areas that are nominally the exclusive domain of the central government. This means evolving an elastic central machinery. With time the process of participation involved in the working together of the various states under an accommodating federal umbrella will gradually teach us how best to stay together. What we need is an arrangement which on the one hand provides a national framework for a possible future strong centre that can operate as such once the important preliminary task of national integration advances far enough, but which on the other hand ensures that we do not play the ostrich in so far as our present-day differences are concerned. Much as we deplore their existence, it is nonetheless true that these differences, when put to the test proved deep enough to produce successive cold-blooded massacres and a horrible civil war in four short years.

For obvious reasons, national strength and solidarity should not be jeopardized by giving undue encouragement to centrifugal forces—a potent risk involved in giving too much power to the states. We should however, avoid the opposite and equally dangerous extreme of providing the temptation for a politically clever minority or section to dominate the country with the excuse of seeking a strong Nigeria. Our aim should be to achieve (a) keeping Nigeria (not a group or a section) strong and (b) ensuring maximum fairness to local interests in a composite and, as yet, inadequately integrated community.

The centre should have all that it *genuinely* needs to keep the country together but we must devise a means to bring to a minimum the risk of abuse of power by the central government.

Our new constitution could be securely founded on a triangular base with the following three sides: (a) an Executive President, representing the nation as a unit and responsible directly to the people; (b) a Senate, representing the interests of the states as units; and (c) a National Assembly, representing party and ideological politics. The National Assembly and the Senate will constitute the Central Legislature.

If the above pattern were to be followed, then the major task before the post-war Constituent Assembly will be to work out an equitable relationship in the spheres of activity between the President, the Senate and the National Assembly. It is in carrying out this delicate exercise that the *Nigerian touch* will come in. It is important that in our search for a constitution we should endeavour to avoid just copying other people's systems. We can certainly borrow a good deal from older institutions but there are rarely any truly identical problems on matters of constitutional arrangements. Older countries evolved their own systems in accordance with their own particular requirements. All we require is the confidence to examine our problems as they are and draw practical conclusions from what we see, while at the same time leaving room for future adjustments as and when the need should arise. This is pragmatism.

General Gowon struck such a pragmatic note on 12th September 1966 in his address to the Ad Hoc Constitutional Conference:

You are required to find what form of political association this great country should adopt. You will find to analyse, *in the light of Nigerian circumstances*, all the arguments for and against all the various types of political arrangements. Two things for the present exercise I feel should be ruled out, viz:
a) complete break-up;
b) a unitary form of government.
   I therefore put before you the following forms of government for consideration:
a) Federal system with a strong central government;
b) Federal system with a weak central government;
c) Confederation, or,
d) An entirely new arrangement which will be peculiar to Nigeria and which has not yet found its way into any political dictionary.[4]

In considering a viable formula for the distribution of responsibilities between the states and the central government, an allied subject of crucial importance is the vexed question of revenue allocation. A committee of experts with equal representation for all the states should be set up to study this sensitive issue. Although our guide should be the joint principle of "derivation and need," past experience has made it abundantly clear that details have to be carefully examined and conflicting interests provided for.

To enhance genuine—not theoretical—participation at the national level and reduce fears of ethnic or sectional domination, central boards, corporations and permanent commissions (Railways, Electricity Corporation of Nigeria, Federal Public Service Commission, the Nigeria Airways, etc.) should have rotating chairmanships. It will also be advisable for members of the Central Court of Appeal to be appointed by the states themselves on a basis of equality and for that chairmanship of that court to rotate among the states. There should be a judicial commission to study the relationship that should exist between a central judiciary and the state judiciaries. Since whatever we achieve now will be largely experimental, there should be provision for an automatic review of the constitution after a ten-year trial period, except of course, that this need not prejudice an earlier review should such a step prove clearly and generally desirable.

Instruments for National Unity

i) An Executive President: A possible shortcut to the solution of our major constitutional problem—dovetailing local and national interests—is an "ambivalent" machinery which can operate simultaneously and harmoniously at two national levels. As already recommended in chapter VIII, I am strongly of the opinion that we would have every advantage in adopting a system in which the central government is headed by a popularly elected Executive President. In addition to taking charge of the "big things"—international relations and the country's overall security —his principal task at home will be that of the guardian of the nation, nursing us carefully from our present childhood to greater national maturity. The states will have the task of reflecting as well as accommodating the realities of our differences and should concentrate on the "small things"—catering to the day to day existence and happiness of the citizens. In this case, the central government and the state governments become complementary.

Our greatest guarantee for success in evolving a national attitude—a common feeling—is the creation of an effective *national personality*. The absence of this personality in the old constitution left the nation with only political factions and parties, none of them possessing any authoritative national image. As the symbol of national unity, he becomes an automatic pole of attraction for national feeling. Because he is distant enough from day to day trivialities, the president will be relatively free from the dirt of local politics. This aloofness makes him a more acceptable umpire in interstate disputes. The method of his election— popular vote—is a guarantee that his interest will be national, not partisan. Because he would have (as I recommended earlier) ultimate control of the armed forces of the entire nation, his intervention in such matters would have to be respected. He will fill the most noticeable gap in the old constitution—creating an institution which combines the opportunity to be objective and fair with the strength to do so.

ii) Education: The most promising field for fruitful cooperation between the central government and the state governments is that of education. Normally, the states will be responsible for general education and will pursue their programmes in accordance with their purse and needs. The help from the central government will be aimed at filling gaps, especially in the budgets of the more needy states. To a large extent this was the pattern followed in the past.

Now is the time for us to exploit education positively as an instrument for national unity. There should be a centrally controlled educational commission to produce and direct a programme to this end. "Integrated schools" should be set up with the fixed objective of teaching the new generation what the present did not learn, and is now too old to absorb—the responsibilities of nationhood in a composite society. Well thought-out programmes should include seminars, excursions, participation in community development projects in states outside the student's own state. All these should be designed to get him involved with the other peoples' problems, thus encouraging a greater psychological integration between him and his fellow countrymen.

Today the vast majority of adult Nigerians know practically nothing about Nigeria or her problems at the national level. For a man born and bred exclusively in Calabar, Badagry, Yola or Kaura-Namoda, the image of Nigeria is nothing more than his own community simply enlarged. Differences of culture, religion, etc., are unknown to him and yet it is upon his proper understanding and appreciation of these differences that national harmony and peace ultimately depend.

Our educational system has to be positively employed in teaching our citizens that although cultural and religious differences exist, their very variety is in fact our richest cultural heritage. Besides being actively encouraged to learn his neighbour's language, the Nigerian schoolboy must be taught, in a larger African context, to consider Usuman Dan Fodio, Jaja of Opobo, Oba Ovarami and Oduduwa as his forefathers. The aim will be to lead him out psychologically from his tribal enclave onto a larger national stage. The Nigerian of tomorrow should aim at becoming a synthesis of the elements inherent in our various cultures. The acquisition of such a combination of qualities will produce "the Nigerian."

Nigeria and Africa's Political Evolution

In an editorial in a special issue of the Paris weekly *Jeune Afrique* devoted to the Nigerian conflict, Tunisia's Bechir Ben Yahmed, a strong advocate of "one Nigeria," wrote as follows:

> Like the Congo after her war against secession, the way is now clear for the emergence of a new and powerful Nigeria. By the time this happens Nigeria will become a real problem for her neighbours in Africa, just as the United States by their immense power are a problem for the rest of America. Then either ourselves or our children will have a great deal to say about *Nigerian imperialism*.[5]

The reference is clear. He was speaking for many of Africa's present day mini-states. Thus an additional but hardly unimportant consideration when looking at Nigeria's future is the possible bearing it can have on the trend of political and economic evolution in our continent.

For many Africans, Nigeria's size and potential strength are a source of fear as well as pride. This is normal. Few people will feel comfortable if they have a potential giant for a neighbour.

Indeed, rightly or wrongly, there are a number of people who held the view that it was the desire to cut Nigeria down to a "safe" size that encouraged some African countries to side with Biafra during the civil war. This point is, of course, a very debatable one but it clearly touches on a sensitive and very real political problem concerning the future.

In the decades ahead inter-African relations will matter to African states very much more than is now the case. So also will the question of greater African cohesion—African unity. In this new setting, the new Nigeria will have a special role to play. By her strength, she could make or mar a great deal.

Africa has not taken final shape. Although the boundaries inherited from colonial powers may have certain advantages, they clearly possess one major disadvantage. This is that ethnic and cultural considerations were totally ignored. The result, as I have attempted to show in earlier chapters, is that neighbouring states contain torn-up patches of different ethnic groups. The Hausa population in the French-speaking Republic of Niger has a much closer cultural affinity with the Hausas of Northern Nigeria than the latter have with the Nupes in the same Northern part of Nigeria. So with the Yorubas split between Dahomey and Nigeria. This is a phenomenon that has marked the history and existence of many African states today. The departure of former colonial masters is still a recent event and many of our present-day leaders are doing no more than maintaining inherited estates. For the time being many factors including illiteracy keep the masses in Africa relatively isolated from active participation in the process of policy making. Only a tiny percent of Africans today have a clear idea of Africa's geography or history. Contact with neighbours is thin and restricted to two levels. The first is a tiny intellectual community that reads the newspapers and follows African politics on a continental plane. The second is a small group of itinerant traders who operate across borders and whose scope of activity and contact with the continent as a whole is limited.

A generation from now, the story is likely to be very different. General education and a higher literacy score among the masses are bound to encourage a wider continental vision. In turn, greater knowledge of the continent and its contents will increasingly expose the artificiality of existing boundaries. A new generation unhampered by the complexes of a colonial past will find such divisions and the artificial economic obstacles they create increasingly unbearable. In short, with that generation will gradually emerge the need for, and therefore a practical approach to, African unity. At that moment, constitutional elasticity in any Nigerian union could become a definite advantage to Africa. A federal union which carefully dovetails the demands of the big nation-state with adequate local freedom for the pursuit of accustomed cultural, religious and social habits will become an elastic bag which can expand effortlessly to admit more states without upsetting any of the original contents. By its accommodating nature, such an arrangement could provide one of the surest bases for a rapid, yet stable and genuine unification of Africa. Potentially, Nigeria offers this base. The artificiality of the present boundaries and the obvious need for greater economic cooperation offer the urge. But no African state will want to be absorbed by a Nigerian colossus.

Today our major worry is how to shed our tribal colour for a national one. Tomorrow, in a world of big-power politics our worry on the African continent—the least populous and the least developed—will become how to work together effectively and harmoniously. Nigeria's current population of fifty-six million is more than half of West Africa's total of some one hundred million. This is to say that Nigeria is actually a "British made" regional union, grouping together as many people as there are in all the other West African countries put together. Squeezing so large and so composite a population too tight too fast appears both unnecessary and unsafe. With a supple and realistic arrangement, making adequate allowance for local differences and local liberty, Nigeria could evolve a "pattern of association" attractive enough to seduce other African countries. Thus Senegal, Ivory Coast, Niger or Cameroun could join that union while retaining their present boundaries and a good deal of their own accustomed administrative setup. Losing nothing or little of their special identities, they have only to gain through the economic advantages accruing from a large internal market and stronger bargaining power vis-à-vis the outside world. Politically, they will benefit from the protection and security which a more powerful state can give. These advantages will attract them only if they feel that in a larger union they are being neither swallowed nor enslaved.

Conclusion

In recommending a supple federal union for Nigeria, as I have attempted to do above, I do not have any illusions about the difficulties that such an idea will encounter. In the first place, I do not regard my recommendation as the only possible path towards political stability for Nigeria. The important point is that I consider it by far the safest path because it allows the multifarious peoples of that country—suddenly brought together to form a modern state only a matter of decades ago by the force of British imperialism—the time they require to learn more about one another.

At present there are many factors that militate against the idea of a Nigerian union with emphasis on greater local autonomy. One such factor is the psychological mood created in Lagos by the decisive victory of the federal forces in the recent civil war. It is not easy to preach compromise and concession to a central authority at a time when it has just begun to feel its new power and authority in the country. Whether or not concessions are ultimately made to local interests, by allowing greater decentralization of political power, will eventually depend on how the Federal Military Government fares in the immediate years ahead. Biafra's secession had the effect of uniting otherwise bitter enemies and sharply opposed interests in a struggle to preserve Nigeria's integrity. In that fight important differences of opinion were submerged. The one question that remains is whether the disappearance of these differences is permanent or only temporary. If the former, a strong central government has a good chance; if the latter, a supple federal union remains the safest course for keeping the country together in tolerable stability.

NOTES

1. *Fume,* no. 1 (the official organ of the *Federated Union of Midwest Students*), (Benin City, Nigeria, 1969), pp. 1-3.
2. *Nigeria 1966,* no. NNPG 114/66/10,000 (Federal Ministry of Information, Lagos, 1967), p. 44.
3. *Daily Times* (Nigeria), 18 January 1966.
4. *Nigeria 1966,* no. NNPG 114/66/10,000, p. 40.
5. Bechir Ben Yahmed, "Les Calcus et Les Sentiments," *Jeune Afrique,* 27 January 1970, p. 35.

Appendixes

MINUTES OF THE SUPREME MILITARY COUNCIL HELD IN GHANA ON 4TH AND 5TH JANUARY 1967[1]

1. The Supreme Military Council held its meeting in Ghana on the 4th-5th January. Those present were:

Lt. Col. Yakubu Gowon: Head of the Federal Military Government.

Colonel Robert Adebayo: Military Governor (West).

Lt. Col. Odumegwu Ojukwu: Military Governor (East).

Lt. Col. David Ejoor: Military Governor (Mid-West).

Lt. Col. Hassan Katsina: Military Governor (North).

Commodore J. E. A. Wey: Head of the Navy.

Major Mobolaji Johnson: Military Administrator of Lagos.

Alhaji Kam Salem: Inspector General of Police.

Mr. J. Omo-Bare: Deputy Inspector General of Police.

Secretaries:

Mr. S. I. A. Akenzua: Permanent Under-Secretary, Federal Cabinet Office.

Mr. P. T. Odumosu: Secretary to the Military Government, West.

Mr. N. U. Akpan: Secretary to the Military Government, East.

Mr. D. P. Lawani: Under-Secretary, Military Governor's Office, Mid-West.

Alhaji Ali Akilu: Secretary to the Military Government, North.

Opening

2. The Chairman of the Ghana National Liberation Council, Lt. General J. A. Ankrah, declaring the meeting open, welcomed the visitors to Ghana and expressed delight that Ghana had been agreed upon by the Nigerian Military Leaders as the venue for this crucial meeting. He considered the whole matter to be the domestic affair of Nigeria, and as such, he refrained from dwelling on any specific points. The General, however, expressed the belief that the Nigerian problems were not such that cannot be easily resolved through patience, understanding and mutual respect. Throughout history, he said, there has been no failure of military statesmen and the eyes of the whole world were on the Nigerian army. He advised that soldiers are purely statesmen and not politicians and the Nigerian Military Leaders owe it as a responsibility to the fifty-six million people of Nigeria to successfully carry through their task of nation-building. Concluding, the General urged the Nigerian Leaders to bury their differences, forget the past and discuss their matter frankly but patiently.

3. Lt. Col. Gowon invited the Nigerian Leaders to say a "joint thank you" to their host, and all said thank you in unison in response to Lt. General Ankrah's address. At this point the General vacated the Conference table.

Importation of Arms and Resolution on the Use of Force

4. Lt. Col. Ojukwu spoke next. He said that the Agenda was acceptable to him subject to the comments he had made on some of the items. (A copy of the Agenda with Lt. Col. Ojukwu's comments is attached to these minutes as Annexure A.) Lt. Col. Ojukwu said that no useful purpose would be served by using the

meeting as a cover for arms build-up and accused the Federal Military Government of having engaged in large-scale arms deals by sending Major Apolo to negotiate for arms abroad. He alleged that the Federal Military Government recently paid £1 million for some arms bought from Italy and now stored up in Kaduna. Lt. Col. Ojukwu was reminded by the Military Governor, North, and other members that the East was indulging in an arms build-up and that the plane carrying arms which recently crashed on the Camerouns border was destined for Enugu. Lt. Col. Ojukwu denied both allegations. Concluding his remarks on arms build-up, Lt. Col. Ojukwu proposed that if the meeting was to make any progress, all the members must at the outset adopt a resolution to renounce the use of force in the settlement of Nigerian dispute.

5. Lt. Col. Gowon explained that as a former Chief of Staff, Army, he was aware of the deficiency in the country's arms and ammunition, which needed replacement. Since the Defence Industries Corporation could not produce these, the only choice was the order from overseas and order was accordingly placed to the tune of £3/4 million. He said to the best of his knowledge the actual amount that had been paid out was only £80,000 for which he signed a cheque on behalf of the General Officer Commanding. The £80 million about which so much noise has been made was nothing but a typographical error in the Customs in recording the payment of £80,000. As to why these arms were sent up to the North, Lt. Col. Gowon referred to lack of storage facilities in Lagos and reminded his Military Colleagues of the number of times arms and ammunition had been dumped in the sea. This was why, he said, it became necessary to use the better storage facilities in Kaduna. The arms and ammunition had not been distributed because they arrived only two weeks previously and have not yet been taken on charge. After exhaustive discussion to which all members contributed and during which Lt. Col. Ejoor pointed out that it would be necessary to determine what arms and ammunition had arrived and what each unit of the

Army had before any further distribution would take place, *the Supreme Military Council unanimously adopted a Declaration proposed by Lt. Col. Ojukwu, that all members:*

a) renounce the use of force as a means of settling the Nigerian crisis;

b) reaffirm their faith in discussions and negotiation as the only peaceful way of resolving the Nigerian crisis; and

c) agree to exchange information on the quantity of arms and ammunition available in each unit of the Army in each Region and in the unallocated stores, and to share out such arms equitably to the various Commands;

d) agree that there should be no more importation of arms and ammunition until normalcy was restored.

The full text of the Declaration which was signed by all members is attached as Annexure B to these minutes.

Reorganization of the Army

6. The Supreme Military Council, having acknowledged the fact that the series of disturbances since January 15th, 1966, has caused disunity in the Army resulting in lack of discipline and loss of public confidence, turned their attention to the question of how best the Army should be reorganized in order to restore that discipline and confidence. There was a lengthy discussion of the subject and when the arguments became involved members retired into secret session. On their return *they announced that agreement had been reached by them on the reorganization, administration and control of the Army on the following lines:*

a) Army to be governed by the Supreme Military Council under a chairman to be known as Commander in Chief of the

Armed Forces and Head of the Federal Military Government.

b) Establishment of a Military Headquarters comprising equal representation from the Regions and headed by a Chief of Staff.

c) Creation of Area Commands corresponding to existing Regions and under the charge of Area Commanders.

d) Matters of policy, including appointments and promotion to top executive posts in the Armed Forces and the Police, to be dealt with by the Supreme Military Council.

e) During the period of the Military Government, Military Governors will have control over Area Commands for internal security.

f) Creation of a Lagos Garrison including Ikeja Barracks.

7. In connection with the reorganization of the Army, the Council discussed the distribution of Military personnel with particular reference to the present recruitment drive. The view was held that general recruitment throughout the country in the present situation would cause great imbalance in the distribution of soldiers. After a lengthy discussion of the subject, *the Council agreed to set up a Military Committee, on which each Region will be represented, to prepare statistics which will show:*

a) Present strength of Nigerian Army;

b) Deficiency in each sector of each unit;

c) The size appropriate for the country and each Area Command;

d) Additional requirement for the country and each Area Command.

The Committee is to meet and report to Council within two weeks from the date of receipt of instructions.

8. *The Council agreed that pending completion of the exercise in paragraph 7 further recruitment of soldiers should cease.*

9. In respect of item 3(*b*) of the Agenda, implementation of the agreement reached on 9th August 1966 it was agreed, after

*a lengthy discussion, that it was necessary for the agreement
reached on 9th August by the delegates of the Regional Governments to be fully implemented.* In particular, it was accepted in
principle that army personnel of Northern origin should return
to the North from the West. It was therefore felt that a crash
programme of recruitment and training, the details of which
would be further examined after the Committee to look into the
strength and distribution of army personnel had reported, would
be necessary to constitute indigenous army personnel in the West
to a majority there quickly.

Non-Recognition by the East of Lt. Col. Gowon as Supreme Commander

10. The question of the non-recognition by the East of Lt.
Col. Gowon as Supreme Commander and Head of the Federal
Military Government was also exhaustively discussed. Lt. Col.
Ojukwu based his objection on the fact, *inter alia,* that no one can
properly assume the position of Supreme Commander until the
whereabouts of the former Supreme Commander Major General
Aguiyi-Ironsi, was known. He therefore asked that the country
be informed of the whereabouts of the Major General and added
that in his view, it was impossible, in the present circumstances,
for any one person to assume any effective central command of
the Nigerian Army. Lt. Col. Ejoor enunciated four principles to
guide the meeting in formulating an answer to the question of
who should be Supreme Commander. These were the:

a) Problem of effective leadership;

b) Crisis of confidence in the Army;

c) Disruption in the present chain of Command;

d) Inability of any soldier to serve effectively in any unit anywhere in the country.

Lt. Col. Gowon replied that he was quite prepared to make an announcement on the matter and regretted that a formal announcement had been delayed for so long but the delay was originally intended to allow time for tempers to cool down. He reminded his colleagues that they already had the information in confidence. After further discussion and following the insistence by Lt. Col. Ojukwu that Lt. Col. Gowon should inform members of what happened to the former Supreme Commander, members retired into secret session and subsequently returned to continue with the meeting after having reached an agreement among themselves.

11. At this point, the meeting adjourned until Thursday, 5th January. The Communique issued at the end of the first day's sitting is attached as Annex D.

The Powers of the Federal Military Government, Vis-A-Vis the Regional Governments

12. When the meeting resumed on the 5th January, it proceded to consider the form of Government best suited to Nigeria in view of what the country has experienced in the past year (1966). *Members agreed that the legislative and executive authority of the Federal Military Government should remain in the Supreme Military Council to which any decision affecting the whole country shall be referred for determination provided that where it is not possible for a meeting to be held the matter requiring determination must be referred to Military Governors for their comment and concurrence. Specifically, the Council agreed that appointments to senior ranks in the Police, Diplomatic and Consular Services as well as appointments to super-scale posts in the Federal Civil Service and the equivalent posts in Statutory Corporations must be approved by the Supreme Military Council.*

The Regional members felt that all the Decrees or provisions of Decrees passed since 15th January 1966 and which detracted from the previous powers and positions of Regional Governments should be repealed if mutual confidence is to be restored. After this issue had been discussed at some length the Council took the following decisions:

> *The Council decided that:*
> (i) *on the reorganization of the Army:*
>> a) *Army to be governed by the Supreme Military Council under a Chairman to be known as Commander in Chief of the Armed Forces and Head of the Federal Military Government.*
>> b) *Establishment of a Military Headquarters comprising equal representation from the Regions and headed by a Chief of Staff.*
>> c) *Creation of Area Commands corresponding to existing Regions and under the charge of Area Commanders.*
>> d) *Matters of policy, including appointments and promotion to top executive posts in the Armed Forces and the Police, to be dealt with by the Supreme Military Council.*
>> e) *During the period of the Military Government, Military Governors will have control over Area Commands for internal security.*
>> f) *Creation of a Lagos Garrison including Ikeja Barracks.*
>
> (ii) *on appointment to certain posts:*
> *The following appointments must be approved by Supreme Military Council:*
>> a) *Diplomatic and Consular posts.*
>> b) *Senior posts in the Armed Forces and the Police.*
>> c) *Super-scale Federal Civil Service and Federal Corporation posts;*

    (iii) *on the functioning of the Supreme Military Council—Any decision affecting the whole country must be determined by the Supreme Military Council. Where a meeting is not possible such a matter must be referred to Military Governors for comment and concurrence;*

    (iv) *that all the Law Officers of the Federation should meet in Benin on the 14th January and list out all the Decrees and provisions of Decrees concerned so that they may be repealed not later than 21st January if possible;*

    (v) *that for at least the next six months, there should be purely a Military Government, having nothing to do whatever with politicians.*

A statement on the Supreme Military Council is attached as Annex C.

Soldiers Involved in Disturbances on 15th January 1966 and Thereafter

13. Members expressed views about the future of those who have been detained in connection with all the disturbances since 15th January 1966 and *agreed that the fate of soldiers in detention should be determined not later than end of January 1967.*

Ad Hoc Constitutional Conference

14. The Council next considered the question of the resumption of the *Ad Hoc* Constitutional Committee and the acceptance of that Committee's recommendations of September 1966. After some exchange of views, *it was agreed that the Ad Hoc Committee should resume sitting as soon as practicable to begin from*

where they left off, and that the question of accepting the unanimous recommendations of September 1966 be considered at a later meeting of the Supreme Military Council.

The Problems of Displaced Persons

15. The Council considered exhaustively the problems of displaced persons, with particular reference to their rehabilitation, employment and property. The view was expressed and generally accepted that the Federal Government ought to take the lead in establishing a National Body which will be responsible for raising and making appeal for funds. Lt. Col. Ojukwu made the point, which was accepted by Lt. Col. Katsina, that in the present situation, the intermingling of Easterners and Northerners was not feasible. After each Military Governor had discussed these problems as they affected his area, *the Council agreed:*

(a) on rehabilitation, that Finance Permanent Secretaries should resume their meeting within two weeks and submit recommendations and that each Region should send three representatives to the meeting;

(b) on employment and recovery of property, that civil servants and Corporation staff (including daily-paid employees) who have not been absorbed should continue to be paid their full salaries until 31st March 1967 provided they have not got alternative employment, and that the Military Governors of the East, West and Mid-West should send representatives (Police Commissioners) to meet and discuss the problem of recovery of property left behind by displaced persons. Lt. Col. Ejoor disclosed that the employment situation in his Region was so acute that he had no alternative but to ask non-Mid-Westerners working in the private sector in his Region to quit and make room for Mid-Westerners repatriated from elsewhere. Lt. Col. Ojukwu stated

that he fully appreciated the problem faced by both the Military Governor, West, and the Military Governor, Mid-West, in this matter and that if in the last resort, either of them had to send the Easterners concerned back to the East, he would understand, much as the action would further complicate the resettlement problem in the East. He assured Council that his order that non-Easterners should leave the Eastern Region would be kept under constant review with a view to its being lifted as soon as practicable.

16. On the question of future meetings of the Supreme Military Council, *members agreed that future meetings will be held in Nigeria at a venue to be mutually agreed.*

17. On the question of Government information media, *the Council agreed that all Government information media should be restrained from making inflammatory statements and causing embarrassment to various Governments in the Federation.*

18. There were other matters not on the Agenda which were also considered among which were the form of Government for Nigeria (reported in paragraph 12 above) and the disruption of the country's economy by the lack of movement of rail and road transport which the Regional Governors agreed to look into.

19. The meeting began and ended in a most cordial atmosphere and members unanimously issued a second and final communique a copy of which is attached to these minutes as Annex E.

20. In his closing remarks the Chairman of the Ghana National Liberation Council expressed his pleasure at the successful outcome of the meeting. . . . The successful outcome of the meeting was then toasted with champagne and the Nigerians took leave of the Ghanaians.

21. The proceedings of the meeting were reported verbatim for each Regional Government and the Federal Government by their respective official reporters and tape-recorded versions were distributed to each Government.

NOTE

1. "The Meeting of the Supreme Military Council held at Aburi, Accra, Ghana, 4-5 January 1967," *Nigerian Crisis*, vol. 6, no. WT 811/267/10,000 (Eastern Regional Government publication), pp. 19-27.

DECREE NO. 8 WHICH IMPLEMENTED THE ABURI AGREEMENTS

The full text of this important decree is published in supplement to Official Extraordinary Gazette No. 16, vol. 54 of 17th March 1967. It is too long to be recited here in full. Below is a summary of its scope and import as published by the Federal Military Government.

1. The main feature of this Decree is the vesting in the Supreme Military Council of both the legislative and executive powers of the Government of the Federation. The Federal Executive Council which has hitherto exercised these powers has now been divested of them and it is henceforth to discharge those functions that are specifically delegated to it by the Supreme Military Council.

2. In the exercise of these legislative and executive powers, the concurrence of the Head of the Federal Military Government and of all the Military Governors is, for the first time, made essential in respect of certain matters which are set out in section 69(6) of the Constitution. These are, to mention a few, matters affecting or relating to trade, commerce, industry, transport, the Armed Forces, the Nigeria Police, Higher Education, and the territorial integrity of a Region and the provisions of the sections listed in the proviso to section 4(1) of the Constitution.

3. On the other hand, the legislative and executive powers of

the Regions have been fully restored and vested in their respective Military Governors. But the provisions of section 86 of the Constitution of the Federation ensure that no Region shall exercise its executive authority so as to impede or prejudice the exercise of the executive authority of the Federation or to endanger the continuance of federal government in Nigeria.

4. The provisions of section 70 of the Constitution of the Federation give powers to the Supreme Military Council to take over the executive and legislative functions of a Regional Government during any period of emergency which might be declared in respect of that Region by the Supreme Military Council, while those of section 71 give the Supreme Military Council power to take appropriate measures against a Region which attempts to secede from the rest of the Federation, or where the executive authority of the Region is being exercised in contravention of section 86 of the Constitution.

5. On the question of amendment to a Regional Constitution, section 5 of the Constitution of the Federation has been suitably modified to the effect that in respect of certain matters mentioned in the section, like the appointment, tenure of office and terms of service of High Court judges, the functions of the Public Service Commission, the establishment of a Consolidated Revenue Fund, etc., any Edict made shall come into operation only with the concurrence of the Supreme Military Council.

6. The Advisory Judicial Committee established under Decree No. 1 of 1966 and which before now tendered advice to the Supreme Military Council regarding appointment of judges all over the Federation has been abolished. Each Military Governor now controls appointment of judges of the High Court of his Region. But the appointment of the jduges of both the Supreme Court of Nigeria and the High Court of Lagos is made the sole responsibility of the Supreme Military Council.

7. All appointments to posts in the super-scale Group 6 and above in the Public Service of the Federation and appointments

to posts of Deputy Commissioner of Police and above in the Nigeria Police Force are now to be made by the Supreme Military Council. The functions formerly discharged under sections 110 and 146 of the Constitution of the Federation by the Federal Public Service Commission and the Police Service Commission respectively are now to that extent limited.

8. Appointments to the offices of Ambassador, High Commissioner and other principal representatives of the Republic in countries other than Nigeria are now, under the Decree, to be made by the Supreme Military Council.

PORTRAITS OF THE PRINCIPAL FIGURES IN THE NIGERIAN CONFLICT

Balewa, Sir Abubakar Tafawa
(assassinated in Lagos on 15th January, 1966)

Sir Abubakar Tafawa Balewa was born in 1912 in the small town of Tafawa Balewa in Bauchi Province of North-Eastern Nigeria. After primary education in Bauchi, he went to Katsina Higher College for five years, qualifying in 1933 as a teacher. He taught at Bauchi Middle School until 1945, then spent a year at the Institute of Education of London University and on his return was appointed Education Officer for Bauchi Province.

As one of the few educated people of his time in the North, he quickly became involved in the politics of that region. Constitutional development in Nigeria brought the need for indigenous legislators and he soon became a member of the first Northern House of Assembly from which he was elected to the Nigerian Legislative Council in Lagos in 1946. A further constitutional change made him in 1952, as Minister of Works, one of the first group of central government ministers. In 1954, he was appointed Minister of Transport. Rapid constitutional development on the eve of independence brought further changes. Thus, as a parliamentary leader of the N.P.C. (Northern Peoples' Congress), the biggest party in the federal parliament, he was appointed in August 1957 as the first Prime Minister of Nigeria.

After the 1959 eve-of-independence elections, Sir Abubakar became on 1st October 1960 the first Prime Minister of independent Nigeria. Surviving a stormy federal election in 1964, he was reappointed Prime Minister, a post which he retained until his assassination in January 1966. Sir Abubakar's period of six years as the head of the government of independent Nigeria weighed heavily on the frail figure of this quiet man. In Nigeria's turbulent and complex politics, he remained a cool figure preoccupied with the problem of holding together the country's 250 ethnic groups.

In September 1957, in his first parliamentary speech as Prime Minister, he made the following declaration, which is characteristic of the man:

> Today, unity is our greatest concern and it is the duty of every one of us to work to strengthen it. Bitterness due to political differences will carry Nigeria nowhere and I appeal to all political leaders throughout the country to try to control their extremists. Nigeria is large enough to accommodate us all in spite of our political differences.[1]

As head of the federal government, Sir Abubakar controlled Nigeria's foreign policy. Outside Nigeria as within it, he was guided by the same sense of moderation. Opposed to extreme and hasty Pan-Africanism, he is remembered as stating at the inaugural meeting of the O.A.U. at Addis Ababa in 1963 that he did not believe in the "African personality"—the firebrand African nationalism as defined by Kwame Nkrumah of Ghana.

Although he was Nigeria's federal Prime Minister, on the purely party political plane, he was always number two in his own party, the N.P.C. Under the shadow of Sir Ahmadu Bello, that party's imperious and aristocratic chief, he never really had a free hand in ordering the affairs of the federal government. Much of the weakness of which his government was frequently accused came from this subordinate status in which his personal opinion and judgment were constantly interfered with by his party boss.

A devout Moslem, popularly known as "Balewa the good,"

Sir Abubakar was a simple man. In a North of feudal Fulani aristocracy, he was born a commoner, belonging to the small Jere tribe (a branch of the Hausa ethnic group) and throughout his life reflected the humility and native shrewdness that this background gave him. His assassination was perhaps the most regretted in Nigeria, where few people had anything against him as a person. He was killed for what he represented officially—the head of a government that had become unpopular with Nigeria's progressives.

Bello, Sir Ahmadu
(assassinated in Kaduna on 15th January, 1966)

Sir Ahmadu Bello, the Sardauna of Sokoto, first Premier of Northern Nigeria, was born on 12th June 1909 in Rabbah, near Sokoto. His father, Ibrahim, the chief of Rabbah, was a grandson of Usuman Dan Fodio, the Fulani religious leader who founded the Sokoto Empire at the beginning of the nineteenth century. After primary education in Sokoto, he attended Katsina Higher College where he was a contemporary of Sir Abubakar Tafawa Balewa. For three years he taught at Sokoto Middle School. Later, he became the district head of Rabbah. Following a local government course in England, he was appointed secretary to the Sokoto Native Authority.

Like many of his contemporaries among the small elite in Northern Nigeria, he quickly became involved with politics, participating actively in the rapid political changes that preceded Nigeria's independence. He was one of the founders of the N.P.C. (Northern Peoples' Congress) in 1949. His princely background in a feudal North gave the Sardauna—a title which means war leader—automatic leadership of the party. Successively regional Minister of Works, of Local Government and Community

Development, he was appointed in 1954 the first Premier of Northern Nigeria. By this time, the fact that his party controlled the vast and dominant Northern region had made him the most powerful political figure in Nigeria. Imperious in manner and gifted with a keen political sense, Sir Ahmadu was to dominate Nigeria's political life until his death in January 1966.

Although his predominant image is one of a feudal Moslem religious leader, he was really first and foremost a politician. His conservatism and near-ostentatious attention to religion were carefully cultivated attitudes calculated to appeal to the realities of the Northern Nigeria of his time. His personal private life and the basic enlightenment of his policies on education and industrialization in the North do not reveal a man opposed to change. By temperament a natural leader, born into a ruling family, he was ambitious for power. The dominance of the North in the old federation left the seat of power in Nigeria in Kaduna, the North's capital. The Sardauna knew this and preferred to keep direct personal control of the North. "I would rather be called the Sultan of Sokoto than the president of Nigeria," he was quoted as saying as late as 1965.

As the leader of the N.P.C., which controlled the federal government from independence in 1960 until the military coup in 1966, it was normally his place to assume the post of federal Prime Minister. This he left to his deputy, Sir Abubakar Tafawa Balewa, whose activities in Lagos he guided all the time by remote control. Personally charming, Sir Ahmadu was admired by many, feared by many more and respected by all. His attachment to the old North, however, and his undisguised attempt to use that region as a base for controlling the whole of Nigeria made him unpopular in the rest of the country. The assassination of this gifted and certainly the most forceful Nigerian politician of his time was a direct attempt to dislodge a man whose grip on the lever of power appeared so strong that it led many idealistic progressives to think that it would be permanent as long as he lived.

Akintola, Chief Samuel Ladoke
(assassinated in Ibadan on 15th January, 1966)

Chief Samuel Ladoke Akintola was born on 6th July 1910, at Ogbomosho in Western Nigeria. After primary and secondary education at Ogbomosho, he worked for some time as editor of the *Nigerian Baptist*, a magazine published by the Protestant religious organization—the Baptist mission in Lagos. Working as a clerk in the Nigerian Railways and then as editor of the *Daily Service*, a Lagos newspaper, he left for England in 1946 where he studied public administration at Oxford and later qualified as a lawyer. He returned to Nigeria in 1949. Like most of his contemporaries with a good education, he was quickly drawn into politics and was a founding member of the Action Group under the leadership of Chief Obafemi Awolowo. As deputy leader of that party, he was for several years leader of the Action Group parliamentary group in the Federal House, where he served as Minister of Health and Minister of Communications and Aviation.

In preparation for independence, scheduled for 1960, the Action Group took a decision that was to change the career of Akintola and the history of that party. Following the 1959 eve-of-independence elections and in order to project the party's image at the national level, Chief Awolowo, the party leader, came to the centre and Chief Akintola took the place he vacated as the Premier of the Western region. As boss of Western Nigeria, Chief Akintola began to consolidate his position and increasingly resented the interference of Chief Awolowo in the affairs of the West Regional Government. Sharp rivalry developed between the two men. In 1962, things came to a head. There was an open clash in the Western Parliament between the supporters of the two leaders. Chief Akintola, supported by the N.P.C.-controlled federal government, won the day. He formed a new party, the N.N.D.P. (Nigerian National Democratic Party) and entered into alliance with the N.P.C.

Chief Akintola's alliance with the conservative N.P.C. was unpopular among the progressives in the country and particularly in his own Western region, where Chief Awolowo's Action Group was still very popular. The regional elections held in October 1965 brought to a fatal climax popular discontent against Chief Akintola's regime. Three months of bloody rioting followed the announcement that his government had won the elections. The chaos was put to an abrupt end by his assassination.

A Yoruba like Chief Awolowo, brilliant and diplomatic, Chief Akintola was widely acknowledged as the most cunning of Nigerian politicians of his day.

Ironsi, General Johnson Thomas Umunakwe Aguiyi- (assassinated in Ibadan on 29th July, 1966)

General Johnson Thomas Umunakwe Aguiyi-Ironsi was born in March 1924 at Umuahia in Eastern Nigeria. After primary education partly in the East and afterwards at Kano in Northern Nigeria, he joined the Nigerian army as a private in 1942. By 1946, he had risen to the rank of company sergeant major. In 1948, he went to Camberley Staff College in England and returned a year later as second lieutenant of the Royal West African Frontier Force. He served first at Accra (Ghana) before being posted to Lagos. Promoted to captain in 1953 and major in 1955, he served as equerry to Queen Elizabeth II during the royal visit to Nigeria in 1956. Promoted to lieutenant colonel in 1960, he was appointed commander of the fifth battalion of the army stationed in Kano, and later in the year was placed at the head of the Nigerian contingent of the United Nations' force in the Congo.

Here he displayed considerable personal valor, enhancing his reputation as a soldier.

From 1961 to 1962, he was the military attaché to the Nigerian High Commission in London during which period he was promoted brigadier. After a course at the Imperial Defence College, he returned to the Congo in 1964 as commander of the entire United Nations peace-keeping force. He returned to Nigeria in 1965 and with the Nigerianization of the army, he was promoted major general and, as the most senior indigenous officer, became head of the Nigerian army.

The coup of January 1966 brought the army to power and, as its head, Ironsi became the head of the Nigerian government. He was first and foremost a soldier. Neither particularly gifted for, nor really interested in, politics, his regime was marked by indecisive action and was overthrown easily after barely seven months. Although power was handed to him as the leader of the forces loyal to the Balewa administration, the government he inherited was a poisoned gift. Acute political differences and tribal distrust made his position untenable. As an Ibo governing in the charged atmosphere that followed the "Ibo coup," the Hausa-Fulani North distrusted him. His attempts at conciliation only made his overthrow easy for his opponents.

Azikiwe, Dr. Nnamdi

Dr. Nnamdi Azikiwe, former President of the Federal Republic of Nigeria, was born on 16th November 1904 at Zungeru, Northern Nigeria, of Ibo parents from Onitsha in Eastern Nigeria. After primary and secondary education in Nigeria, he studied history and political science in the United States. Returning to Africa in 1934, he spent three years as editor of the *African Morning Post* in Accra (Ghana). He settled in Lagos in 1937 and established a chain of newspapers, the most notable among which was the *West African Pilot.*

He entered politics and was a foundation member of the N.C.N.C. (National Council for Nigerian Citizens) of which he was first secretary-general, becoming its president in 1946.[2] After holding various political and ministerial appointments, he became the first premier of Eastern Nigeria in 1954. First president of the national senate, he became at independence in 1960 governor-general and commander in chief of the Federation of Nigeria. Following further constitutional change, he became president of the new Republic of Nigeria in 1963, a post he held till the military coup in January 1966.

In the confusion and insecurity which followed the coups and massacres of 1966, Dr. Azikiwe fled to his home in Eastern Nigeria where he was overtaken by the secession of Biafra. Never an enthusiast of secession, he served reluctantly in an undefined capacity on a number of missions abroad for the Biafran regime. Breaking with Ojukwu on the question of a negotiated settlement, he went into voluntary exile in London in September 1968. A year later, he came out openly for a peaceful settlement on the basis of a united Nigeria.

Blending academics with politics, Dr. Azikiwe is a very learned man who has published many books on African history and politics. He is the founder of the University of Nigeria at Nsukka, Eastern Nigeria. Popularly known as Zik of Africa, Azikiwe's career from the start has been marked by a strong Pan-African flavour. It is perhaps this continental vision, more than anything else, that ultimately decided his adherence to the principle of preserving one Nigeria.

> As a young man I saw visions. I do not doubt that as an old man, I shall dream dreams. Some of the dreams must be of my relentless struggle for the peoples of Africa, and for the cause of Nigerian freedom and unity.[2]

A convinced and scrupulous constitutionalist, a democrat "almost to a fault," as an admirer once said, Dr. Azikiwe is a rare bird in the rough and strong-armed politics of today's Africa.

Awolowo, Chief Obafemi

Chief Obafemi Awolowo, former leader of the Action Group, was born at Ijebu-Remu on the 6th of March 1909. The son of a Yoruba farmer, he is one of the truly self-made men among his Nigerian contemporaries.

During a checkered career as a teacher, shorthand typist, businessman, newspaper reporter and then trade unionist, he studied in his spare time, gaining a bachelor's degree in commerce in 1944. He entered Nigerian politics briefly before going to England to qualify as a lawyer in 1947. On his return he plunged into politics and in 1951 founded the Action Group. After serving in various ministerial capacities, he became premier of the Western Region in 1954. At independence in 1960, he quit that post to become leader of opposition in the Federal Parliament. A tussle for power between him and his deputy, Chief S. L. Akintola, who replaced him as premier of the Western Region, and his rigid opposition to the N.P.C.-controlled Federal Government brought an alliance of his enemies which soon led to his trial and imprisonment on charges of treason in 1963. He was released by General Gowon soon after the military coup of July 1966.

A popular leader among the progressives in prewar Nigeria Chief Awolowo attempted in vain to bring about a last minute reconciliation between General Gowon and General Ojukwu. On this account he led a peace delegation to Enugu (Ojukwu's capital) in early May 1967. When Biafra seceded and war broke out, he gave his support to General Gowon and was appointed to the highest civilian post in the Federal Military Government—the vice-presidency of the Federal Executive Council. Strong-

willed, austere and single-minded, Chief Awolowo, who has published a number of books on Nigerian politics and constitution,
is perhaps the boldest and certainly one of the most ruthless of
Nigeria's politicians.

Gowon, Major General Yakubu

Major General Yakubu Gowon was born on 19th October 1934
in Pankshin district of Plateau Province in Northern Nigeria. The
son of a Methodist minister from the small Anga tribe, General
Gowon was brought up a Christian amidst the predominantly
Moslem community of Northern Nigeria. After primary educa-
tion in a mission school, he went to Government College in
Zaria, to the Regular Officers Special Training School in Teshie
(Ghana), then to Eton Hall and Sandhurst Military Academy in
England. Back in Nigeria, he was appointed second lieutenant in
1957. After service at the military headquarters and the Southern
Cameroons (then part of Nigeria), he served with the United
Nations' forces in the Congo in 1960, by which time he was
already a major. In 1962, he attended a course at the Army Staff
College in Camberley, England. In 1963, he was promoted lieutenant colonel and in May 1965 he returned to England for a
course at the Joint Services Staff College at Lartimer, Bucking-
hamshire. He returned to Nigeria only on 13th January 1966, two
days before the coup—a late arrival that possibly excluded him
from the list of victims. With the military in power, General
Ironsi appointed him Chief of Staff of the Nigerian army. Seven
months later, when the July coup brought him to the head of the
Federal Military Government, he took the title of major general.

Coming from a minority ethnic group and moderate in temperament, General Gowon, but for his uniform, presents the
peaceful image of Abubakar Tafawa Balewa. This moderation
was perhaps the greatest single asset that gave him victory over

Biafran secession. He was able to convince many outsiders that he was fighting the civil war against his will. Within Nigeria, it helped him in the long run to secure the support of moderate Ibos, like Dr. Azikiwe, anxious to put an end to bloodshed and mass suffering.

Ojukwu, Major General Chukwuemeka Odumegwu

Major General Chukwuemeka Odumegwu Ojukwu was born on 4th November 1933 at Zungeru, Northern Nigeria. His father, Sir Louis Odumegwu Ojukwu started life as a small businessman from Nnewi in Eastern Nigeria and, making intelligent use of the boom in the transport business during World War II, made himself one of the richest men in Nigeria by the time he died in September 1966.

After primary school in Lagos, young Emeka was sent at thirteen by his father to Epsom College in England. At eighteen, he left Epsom for Lincoln College, Oxford, where he obtained a bachelor's degree in modern history. He returned to Nigeria in 1956 and after a short spell as an administrative officer, he joined the Nigerian army in 1957. His background and education made promotion quick and, after service in the Congo, he was promoted to lieutenant colonel in 1964. He was in charge of the fifth battalion of the Nigerian army stationed in Kano at the time of the coup of January 1966. In spite of pleas for his support from the coup's leader, Major Nzeogwu, he threw his lot with the loyal forces under General Ironsi who soon afterwards appointed him Military Governor of Eastern Nigeria. The tension and bitterness which followed the massacres of Ibos in September 1966 led to his decision on 30th May 1967 to secede from the Federation of Nigeria.

He called his new state Biafra and became its head. Secession was followed by civil war. For thirty months, Ojukwu, who now took the title of major general, fought tenaciously against overwhelming odds to defend the sovereignty of his state. When Biafra collapsed in January 1970, he fled to the Ivory Coast, where he was granted political asylum.

Intelligent, proud and perhaps over-ambitious, he proved too rigid a leader to accept moderate advice and, despite a prolonged military stalemate, was unable to seek timely compromise and end the war by negotiation.

NOTES

1. *Nigeria Speaks. Speeches by Sir Abubakar Tafawa Balewa* (Longmans Green, 1964), p. 6.
2. Formerly the National Council for Nigeria and the Cameroons. The name was changed in 1960 when the Cameroons left Nigeria.
3. *Zik. A Selection from the Speeches of Dr. Nnamdi Azikiwe.* (London, 1961), p. viii.

INDEX